Starting and Scaling DevOps in the Enterprise

Gary Gruver

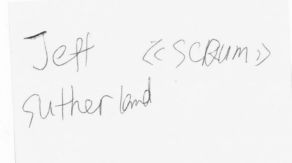

Print ISBN: 978-1-48358-358-7

eBook ISBN: 978-1-48358-359-4

Elephant pictures by Amelia Tiedemann

Graphics by Shahla Mahdavi and Cassie Lydon of Katie Bush design

TABLE OF CONTENTS

ABOUT THE AUTHOR

Gary Gruver is an experienced executive with a proven track record of transforming software development and delivery processes in large organizations, first as the R&D director of the LaserJet firmware group that completely transformed how they developed embedded firmware and then as VP of QA, Release, and Operations at Macy's.com where he led the journey toward continuous delivery. He now consults with large organizations and runs workshops to help them transform their software development and delivery processes. He is the co-author of *Leading the Transformation: Applying Agile and DevOps Principles at Scale* and *A Practical Approach to Large-Scale Agile Development: How HP Transformed LaserJet FutureSmart Firmware.*

Website: GaryGruver.com

Twitter: @GRUVERGary

Linkedin: https://www.linkedin.com/in/garygruver

Email: gary@garygruver.com

ACKNOWLEDGMENTS

Many people have contributed to this book. I would like to thank everyone I have worked with over the years who helped me better understand how to develop software. The ideas shared in this book are an accumulation of everything I have learned from working with each of you on a constant journey of improving software development processes. Without these discussions and debates, my understanding would not be as rich and the book would not be as complete.

I would like to especially thank all the clients of the executive and execution workshops for letting me join you on your journey. Sharing the challenges you were facing and the improvements that worked helped to fine tune the content of this book. Thanks also to Paul Remeis and Greg Lonnon for helping to fine tune the content by helping me deliver and improve the execution workshops.

I would like to thank everyone that has taken time to give me feedback on early versions of the book (in alphabetical order): John Ediger, Mirco Hering, Jez Humble, Tommy Mouser, and Vinod Peris. Your input significantly improved the final product.

I would also like to thank the editorial and production staff: Kate Sage, the editor, did a great job of forcing me to clarify the ideas so they could be communicated clearly and concisely. The back and forth made for a better book, but more importantly it required me to crisp up the concepts, enabling me to be more efficient at helping others on their journeys. Shahla Mahdavi and Cassie Lydon from Katie Bush design provided most of the graphics. They did a great job if creating visual artifacts to help communicate the ideas I am trying to get across. Finally, I would like to thank Amelia Tiedemann for the wonderful elephant pictures and cover design. I feel she was really helpful in communicating that a successful DevOps transformation requires more than just having all the right parts.

FORWARD

When David Farley and I wrote the Continuous Delivery book, we thought we were tackling a dusty, niche corner of the software delivery lifecycle. We didn't expect a huge amount of interest in the book, but we were sick of seeing people spending weeks getting builds deployed into testing environments, performing largely manual regression testing that took weeks or months, and spending their nights and weekends getting releases out of the door, often accompanied by long outages. We knew that much of the software delivery process was hugely inefficient, and produced poor outcomes in terms of the quality and stability of the systems produced. We could also see from our work in large enterprises that the tools and practices existed that would remove many of these problems, if only teams would implement them systematically.

Fortunately, we weren't the only ones who saw this. Many others—including Gary—had come to the same conclusion across the world, and the DevOps movement was born. This movement has had unprecedented success, primarily because these ideas work. As I've worked with leaders in large, regulated companies, and most recently as a US federal government employee at 18F, I've seen order of magnitude improvements in delivery lead times accompanied by improvements in quality and resilience, even when working with complex, legacy systems.

Most important of all, I've seen these ideas lead to happier technology workers and end users. Using continuous delivery, we can build products whose success derives from a collaborative, experimental approach to product development. Everybody in the team contributes to discovering how to produce the best user and organizational outcomes. End users benefit enormously when we can work with them from early on in the delivery process and iterate rapidly, changing the design of systems in response to their feedback, and delivering the most important features from early on in the product lifecycle.

Gary has been applying ideas from the Continuous Delivery and DevOps playbook from well before these terms became popular, starting with his work at HP leading the FutureSmart LaserJet Firmware team. His large, distributed team applied continuous delivery to printer firmware, and showed the transformational results this created in terms of quality and productivity in a domain where nobody cared about frequent deployments. Then he went on to do the same thing in a regulated organization with complex, tightly coupled legacy systems.

Today's technology leaders understand the urgency of transforming their organizations to achieve both better quality and higher productivity. Effective leadership is essential if these kinds of transformation are to succeed. However overcoming the combined obstacles of organizational inertia, silo-based thinking and high levels of architectural complexity can seem like an overwhelming task. This book provides a concise yet thorough guide to the engineering practices and architectural change that is critical to achieving these breakthrough results, from a leader's perspective.

This book won't make your journey easy—but it will serve as an invaluable map to guide your path. Happy travels!

Jez Humble

Chapter 1

DEVOPS AND THE DEPLOYMENT PIPELINE

Software is starting to play a much larger role in how companies compete across a broad range of industries. As the basis of competition shifts to software, large traditional organizations are finding that their current approaches to managing software are limiting their ability to respond as quickly as the business requires. DevOps is a fundamental shift in how leading edge companies are starting to manage their software and IT work. It is driven by the need for businesses to move more quickly and the realization that large software organizations are applying these DevOps principles to develop new software faster than anyone ever thought possible. Everyone is talking about DevOps.

In my role, I get to meet lots of different companies, and I realized quickly that DevOps means different things to different people. They all want to do "DevOps" because of all the benefits they are hearing about, but they are not sure exactly what DevOps is, where to start, or how to drive improvements over time. They are hearing a lot of different great ideas about DevOps, but they struggle to get everyone to agree on a common definition and what changes they should make. It is like five blind men describing an elephant. In large organizations, this lack of alignment on DevOps improvements impedes progress and leads to a lack of focus. This book is intended to help structure and align those improvements by providing a framework that large organizations and their executives can use to understand the DevOps principles in the context of their current development processes and to gain alignment across the organization for successful implementations.

Part of the issue with implementing DevOps principles and practices is that there are so many ideas out there about what DevOps is, and so many different ways to define it. The most consistent and comprehensive definition I have heard lately is from Gene Kim, a co-author of The Phoenix Project and The DevOps Handbook. He is a great thought leader and evangelist for the DevOps movement. In order to get us all on the same page for our work here, we will use his definition of DevOps:

> DevOps should be defined by the outcomes. It is those sets of cultural norms and technology practices that enable the fast flow of planned work from, among other things, development through tests into operations, while preserving world class reliability, operation, and security. DevOps is not about what you do, but what your outcomes are. So many things that we associate with DevOps, such as communication and culture, fit underneath this very broad umbrella of beliefs and practices.

People have such different views of DevOps because what it takes to improve quality and flow at every step, from a business idea all the way out to working code in the customer's hands, differs for different organizations. The DevOps principles designed to improve this process are a lot about implementing changes that help coordinate the work across teams. The movement started with leading edge, fairly small companies that were delivering code more frequently than anyone thought possible. DevOps was also very successful in large organizations like Amazon where they re-architected their monolithic system to enable small teams to work independently. More recently, DevOps has started being leveraged into large organizations with tightly coupled architectures that require coordinating the work across hundreds of people. As it started scaling into these larger more complex organizations, the problem was that people started assuming the approaches for successfully coordinating the work across small teams would be the same and work as well for coordinating the work across large organizations. The reality is that while the principles are the same for small and complex, the implementations can and should be different.

Most large organizations don't have that context as they start their DevOps journey. They have different people in different roles who have gone to different conferences to learn about DevOps from presentations by companies with different levels of complexity and different problems and have come back with different views of what DevOps means for them, like when the five blind men describe the elephant. Each stakeholder gives a very accurate description of their section of the DevOps elephant, but the listener never gets a very good macro view of DevOps. So, when they go to create their own elephant, nobody can agree on where to start, and they frequently want to implement ideas that worked well for small teams, but are not designed for complex organizations that require coordinating the work of hundreds of people. The intent of this book is to provide the overall view of the elephant to help large organizations gain a common understanding of the concepts and provide a framework they can use to align the organization on where to start and how to improve their software development processes over time.

This is important because if you can't get people in a large organization aligned on both what they are going to build and what approach they are going to use for prioritizing improvement, they are not very likely to deliver a DevOps implementation that will deliver the expected results. It will potentially have pieces of the different things that the organization has heard about DevOps, but it won't really help the organization deliver code on a more frequent basis while improving or maintaining all aspects of quality. It is like having the five blind men build an elephant based on their understanding of the animal. It may have all the right parts, but it doesn't really look like or work like an elephant because they don't have a good macro view of the animal.

To clarify the macro view of DevOps, we will look at how a business idea moves to development, where a developer writes code, through the creation of the environment to how code gets deployed, tested, and passed into production where it is monitored. The process of moving from a business idea all the way out to the customer using a deployment pipeline (DP) was originally documented by Jez Humble and David Farley in their book Continuous Delivery. This book will leverage that framework extensively because I believe it represents the basic construct of DevOps. It captures the flow of business ideas to the customer and the quality gates that are required to maintain or improve quality.

It is my personal experience that creating, documenting, automating, and optimizing DPs in large software/IT organizations is key to improving their efficiency and effectiveness. You already have in place something that you are using to get code through your organization from idea to production, which is your DP. But documenting that so everyone has a common view and optimizing it based on using value stream mapping is a key tool in this process that helps to align the organization. The DP defines and documents the flow of code through the system, and value stream mapping the DP helps to identify bottlenecks and waste and other inefficiencies that can be addressed using DevOps techniques. Improving it will require a lot of organizational change management, but the DP will help everyone understand what processes are being changed at any one time and how they should start working differently.

The DP for a large organization with a tightly coupled architecture is a fairly complex concept to grasp. Therefore, in Chapter 2, we will start with the simplest example of a DP with one developer and will show the inefficiencies that can occur with one developer. Then, in Chapter 3, we will highlight the DevOps approaches that were designed to address those issues. We will also show the metrics you can start collecting to help you understand the magnitude of your inefficiencies so you can align your organization on fixing the issues that will provide the biggest benefit.

Once the basic construct of the DP is well understood, in Chapter 4 we will show how the complexity changes as you start scaling the DP from one developer to a team of developers. Having a team of developers working together on an application while keeping it close to release quality is a fundamental shift for most traditional organizations. It requires some different technical approaches by the developers, but it also requires a cultural shift that prioritizes keeping the code base stable over creating new features. This will be a big shift for most organizations, but it is very important because if you can't get the developers to respond to the feedback from the DP, then creating it will be of limited value.

The next big challenge large organizations have after they have had some success at the team level concerns how to scale DevOps across a large organization. They typically approach it by trying to get the rest of the organization to do what they did because of the benefits it provided. This overlooks the fact that the biggest barriers to adoption are not technical, but instead involve organizational change management and getting people to work differently. The key to this adoption is helping the broader organization understand the principles, while providing as much flexibility as possible to allow them to develop and take ownership of their plans. In order to make this adoption of principles as flexible as possible, in Chapter 5 we will cover how to segment the work in large organizations into the smallest pieces possible to enable local control and ownership. For some organizations with loosely coupled architectures, this will result in a lot of small, independent teams where you only have to coordinate the work across tens of people. For other organizations with tightly coupled architectures that require large applications to be developed, qualified, and released together, this will require coordinating the work across hundreds of people. It is important to start by grouping applications into these types because the things you do to coordinate the work across tens of people will be different than the types of things you do to coordinate the work across hundreds of people. While small teams will always be more efficient and deploy more frequently, the process of documenting, automating, and continually improving DPs is much more important for coordinating work across hundreds of people because the inefficiencies across large organizations are much more pronounced.

In Chapter 6, we will provide a quick overview of the approaches that work well for large organizations with small teams that can work independently. This topic will not be covered in a lot of detail because most available DevOps material already covers this very well. In Chapter 7, we will start addressing the complexities of designing a DP for large, tightly-coupled systems. We will show how to break the problem into smaller more manageable pieces and then build those up into more complex releasable systems. In Chapter 8, we cover how to start optimizing these complex DPs, including metrics, to help focus changes in the areas where they will most help the flow through the system. In Chapter 9, we will review and highlight the differences between implementing improvements for small independent teams and for large complex systems.

Changing how a large organization works is going to take a while, and it is going to require changing how everyone both thinks about and does their actual work. A couple of things are important to consider when contemplating this type of organizational change: first, start where it provides the most benefit so you can build positive momentum, and second, find executives that are willing to lead the change and prioritize improvements that will optimize the DP instead of letting teams sub-optimize their segment of the DP.

Once the DP is in place, it provides a very good approach for transforming how you manage large and complex software projects. Instead of creating lots of management processes to track progress and align different teams, you use working code as the forcing function that aligns the organization. Requiring all the different Development teams to integrate their code on a regular basis and ensure it is working with automated testing forces them to align their software designs without a lot of management overhead.

The move to infrastructure as code, which was spearheaded by Jez Humble and David Farley and involves treating all aspects of the software development process with the same of rigor as application code, provided some major breakthroughs. It requires that the process for creating environments, deploying code, and managing databases be automated with code that is documented and tracked in a source code management (SCM) tool just like the application code. This move to infrastructure as code forces a common definition of environments and deployment processes across Development, QA, and Operations teams and ensures consistency on the path to production. Here again it is working code that helps to align these different groups.

Moving to infrastructure as code increases direct communication between Development and Operations, which is key to the success of all sorts of cultural and structural shifts DevOps requires. People no longer log on to computers and make changes that can't be tracked. Instead they work together on common scripts for making changes to the infrastructure that can be tracked in SCM tool. This requires them, at minimum, to document any changes they are making so everyone can see what they are doing, and ideally it forces them to communicate directly about the changes they are making so they can ensure those changes will work in every stage in the DP all the way out to production. Having to use common code and common tools forces the collaboration. The effect that this collaboration has on efficiency cannot be underestimated. Since the teams are aligned by having to ensure their code works together on a daily basis, management processes do not need to be put in place to address those issues. Software is notoriously hard to track well with management processes. Getting status updates everywhere doesn't work that well and takes a lot of overhead. It is more efficient if the teams resolve issues in real time. Additionally, it is much easier to track progress using the DP because instead of creating lots of different managerial updates, everyone can track the progress of working code as it moves down the pipeline.

This approach of a rigorous DP with infrastructure as code and automated testing gating code progression is significantly different from the approach ITIL uses for configuration management. Where the ITIL processes were designed to ensure predictability and stability, the DevOps changes have been driven by the need to improve speed while maintaining stability. The biggest changes are around configuration management and approval processes. The ITIL approach has very strict manual processes for any changes that occur in the configuration of production. These changes are typically manually documented and approved in a change management tool with tickets. The approved changes are then manually implemented in production. This approach helped improve stability and consistency, but slowed down flow by requiring lots of handoffs and manual processes. The DevOps approach of infrastructure as code with automated testing as gates in the DP enables better control of configuration and more rigors in the approval process, while also dramatically improving speed. It does this by automating the process with code and having everything in the SCM tool. The code change being proposed is documented by the script change in the SCM. The approval criteria for accepting the change is documented by automated tests that are also in the SCM. Additionally, you know exactly what change was implemented because it was done with the automation code under revision control. The whole approach puts everything required for change management in one tool with automation that is much easier and quicker to track. It also improves the rigors in the approval processes by requiring the people who traditionally approve the changes to document their criteria via automated tests instead of just using some arbitrary management decision for each change.

This approach provides some huge benefits for auditing and regulatory compliance. Where before the audit team would have to track the manual code changes, approval processes, and implementations in different tools, it is now all automated and easily tracked in one place. It dramatically improves compliance because computers are much better than humans at ensuring the process is followed every time. It is also easier for the auditing team because all the changes are documented in a (SCM) tool that is designed for automatically tracking and documenting changes.

These changes are dramatically improving the effectiveness of large organizations because they improve the flow of value while maintaining stability. Most importantly, though, is that setting up and optimizing a DP requires removing waste and inefficiencies that have existed in your organization for years. In order to improve the flow, you will end up addressing lots of inefficiencies that occur in coordinating work across people. The productivity of individuals will be improved by better quality and faster feedback while they are writing code, but the biggest benefits will come from addressing the issues coordinating the work within teams, across teams, and across organizations. It will require technical implementations and improvement, but by far the biggest challenge is getting people to embrace the approaches and change how they work on a day-to-day basis. These changes will be significant, but the benefits will be dramatic.

Summary

As software becomes the basis of competition, how we currently manage software limits the kinds of quick responses that businesses require. This is where DevOps steps in. It is all about improving speed while maintaining all aspects of quality. As businesses embark on DevOps journeys, though, they are finding that there are myriad ideas out there about what DevOps is and how it is defined. As this book will address, most large organizations don't have a good framework for putting all these different ideas into context as they start their DevOps journey. This makes it difficult to get everyone working together on changes that will improve the end-to-end system. People working in a large organization need to be aligned on what they are going to build and need to find ways to prioritize improvement or else they won't implement DevOps in ways that will deliver the expected results. As this book will show, documenting, automating, and optimizing DPs in large software/IT organizations improves efficiency and effectiveness and offers a very good approach for transforming how you manage large and complex software projects.

Chapter 2

THE BASIC DEPLOYMENT PIPELINE

The DP in a large organization can be a complex system to understand and improve. Therefore, it makes sense to start with a very basic view of the DP, to break the problem down into its simplest construct and then show how it scales and becomes more complex when you use it across big, complex organizations. The most basic construct of the DP is the flow of a business idea to development by one developer through a test environment into production. This defines how value flows through software/IT organizations, which is the first step to understanding bottlenecks and waste in the system. Some people might be tempted to start the DP at the developer, but I tend to take it back to the flow from the business idea because we should not overlook the amount of requirements inventory and inefficiencies that waterfall planning and the annual budgeting process drive into most organizations.

The first step in the pipeline is communicating the business idea to the developer so they can create the new feature. Then, once the new feature is ready, the developer will need to test it to ensure that it is working as expected, that the new code has not broken any existing functionality, and that it has not introduced any security holes or impacted performance. This requires an environment that is representative of production. The code then needs to be deployed into the test environment and tested. Once the testing ensures the new code is working as expected and has not broken any other existing functionality, it can be deployed into production, tested, and released. The final step is monitoring the application in production to ensure it is working as expected. In this chapter, we will review each step in this process, highlighting the inefficiencies that frequently occur. Then, in Chapter 3, we will review the DevOps practices that were developed to help address those inefficiencies.

Requirements

The first step in the DP is progressing from a business idea to work for the developer to create the new feature. This usually involves creating a requirement and planning the development to some extent. The first problem large organizations have with flow of value through their DP is that they tend to use waterfall planning. They do this because they use waterfall planning for every other part of their business so they just apply the same processes to software. Software, however, is unlike anything else most organizations manage in three ways. First, it is much harder to plan accurately because everything you are asking your teams to do represents something they are being asked to do it for the first time. Second, if software is developed correctly with a rigorous DP, it is relatively quick and inexpensive to change. Third, as an industry we are so poor at predicting our customers' usage that over 50% of all software developed is never used or does not meet its business intent. Because of these unique characteristics of software, if you use waterfall planning, you end up locking in your most flexible and valuable asset in order to deliver features that won't ever be used or won't deliver the intended business results. You also use up a significant amount of your capacity planning instead of delivering real value to your business.

Organizations that use waterfall planning also tend to build up lots of requirements inventory in front of the developer. This inventory tends to slow down the flow of value and creates waste and inefficiencies in the process. As the Lean manufacturing efforts have clearly demonstrated, wherever you have excess inventory in the system tends to drive waste in terms of rework and expediting. If the organization has invested in creating the requirements well ahead of when they are needed, when the developer is ready to engage, the requirement frequently needs to be updated to answer any questions the developer might have and/or updated to respond to changes in the market. This creates waste and rework in the system.

The other challenge with having excess inventory of requirements in front of the developer is that as the marketplace evolves, the priorities should also evolve. This leads to the organization having to reprioritize the requirements on a regular basis or, in the worst case, sticking to a committed plan and delivering features that are less likely to meet the needs of the current market. If these organizations let the planning process lock them into committed plans, it creates waste by delivering lower value features. If the organizations reprioritize a large inventory of requirements, they will likely deprioritize requirements that the organization has invested a lot of time and energy in creating. Either way, excess requirements inventory leads to waste.

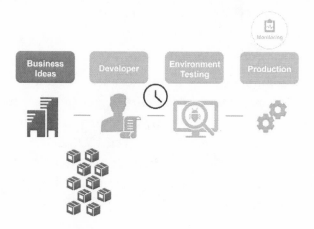

Test Environment

The next step is getting an environment where the new feature can be deployed and tested. The job of providing environments typically belongs to Operations, so they frequently lead this effort. In small organizations using the cloud, this can be very straightforward and easy. In large organizations using internal datacenters, this can be a very complex and timely process that requires working through extensive procurement and approval processes with lengthy handoffs between different parts of the organization. Getting an environment can start with long procurement cycles and major operational projects just to coordinate the work across the different server, storage, networking, and firewall teams in Operations. This is frequently one of the biggest pain points that cause organizations to start exploring DevOps.

There is one large organization that started their DevOps initiative by trying to understand how long it would take to get up Hello World! in an environment using their standard processes. They did this to understand where the biggest constraints were in their organization. They quit this experiment after 250 days even though they still did not have Hello World! up and running because they felt they had identified the biggest constraints. Next, they ran the same experiment in Amazon Web Services and showed it could be done in two hours. This experiment provided a good understanding of the issues in their organization and also provided a view of what was possible.

Testing and Defect Fixing

Once the environment is ready, the next step is deploying the code with the new feature into the test environment and ensuring it works as expected and does not break any existing functionality. This step should also ensure that there were no security or performance issues created by the new code. Three issues typically plague traditional organizations at this stage in their DP: repeatability of test results, the time it takes to run the tests, and the time it takes to fix all the issues.

Repeatability of the results is a big source of inefficiency for most organizations. They waste time and energy debugging and trying to find code issues that end up being problems with the environment, the code deployment, or even the testing process. This makes it extremely difficult to determine when the code is ready to flow into production and requires a lot of extra triaging effort for the organization. Large, complex, tightly coupled organizations frequently spend more time setting up and debugging these environments than they do writing code for the new capabilities.

This testing is typically done with expensive and time-consuming manual tests that are not very repeatable. This is why it's essential to automate your testing. The time it takes to run through a full cycle of manual testing delays the feedback to developers, which results in slow rework cycles, which reduces flow in the DP. The time and expense of these manual test cycles also forces organizations to batch lots of new features together into major releases, which slows the flow of value and makes the triage process more difficult and inefficient.

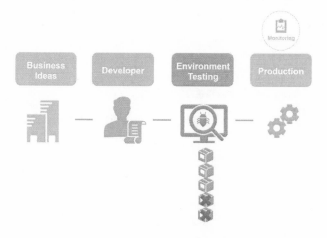

The next challenge in this step is the time and effort it takes to remove all the defects from the code in the test environment and to get the applications up to production level quality. In the beginning, the biggest constraint is typically the time it takes to run all the tests. When this takes weeks, the developers can typically keep up with fixing defects at the rate at which the testers are finding them. This changes once the organization moves to automation where all the testing can be run in hours, at which point the bottleneck tends to move toward the developers ability to fix all the defects and get the code to production levels of quality.

Once an organization gets good at providing environments or is just adding features to an application that already has environments set up, reaching production level quality is frequently one of the biggest challenges to releasing code on a more frequent basis. I have worked with organizations that have the release team leading large cross-organizational meetings to get applications tested, fixed, and ready for production. They meet every day to review the testing progress to see when it will be done so they are ready to release to production. They track all the defects and fixes so they can make sure the current builds have production level quality. Frequently, you see these teams working late on a Friday night to get the build ready for offshore testing over the weekend only to find out Saturday morning that all the offshore teams were testing with the wrong code or a bad deployment, or the environment was misconfigured in some way. This process can drive a large amount of work into the system and is so painful that many organizations choose to batch very large, less frequent releases to limit the pain.

Production Deployment

Once all the code is ready, the next step is to deploy the code into production for testing and release to the customer. Production deployment is an Operations led effort, which is important because Operations doesn't always take the lead in DevOps transformations, but when you use the construct of the DP to illustrate how things work, it becomes clear that Operations is essential to the transformation and should lead certain steps to increase efficiency in the process. It is during this step that organizations frequently see issues with the application for the first time during the release. It is often not clear if these issues are due to code, deployment, environments, testing, or something else altogether. Therefore, the deployment of large complex systems frequently requires large cross-organizational launch calls to support releases. Additionally, these deployment processes themselves can require lots of time and resources for manual implementations. The amount of time, effort, and angst associated with this process frequently pushes organizations into batching large amounts of change into less frequent releases.

Monitoring and Operations

Monitoring is typically another Operations-led effort since they own the tools that are used to monitor production. Frequently, the first place in the DP that monitoring is used is in production. This is problematic because when code is released to customers, developers haven't been able to see potential problems clearly before the customer experience highlights it. If Operations works with Development to move monitoring up the pipeline, potential problems are caught earlier and before they impact the customer.

When code is finally released to the customers and monitored to ensure it is working as expected, then ideally there shouldn't be any new issues caught with monitoring in production if all the performance and security testing was complete with good coverage. This is frequently not the case in reality. For example, I was part of one large release into production where we had done extensive testing going through a rigorous release process, only to have it immediately start crashing in production as a result of an issue we had never seen before. Every time we pointed customer traffic to the new code base, it would start running out of memory and crashing. After several tries and collecting some data, we had to spend several hours rolling back to the old version of the applications. We knew where the defect existed, but even as we tried debugging the issues, we couldn't reproduce it in our test environments. After a while, we decided we couldn't learn any more until we deployed into production and used monitoring to help locate the issue. We deployed again, and the monitoring showed us that we were running out of memory and crashing. This time the developers knew enough to collect more clues to help them identify the issue. It turns out a developer was fixing a bug that was not wrapping around a long line of text correctly. The command the developer had used worked fine in all our testing, but in production we realized that IE8 localized to Spanish had a defect that would turn this command into a floating point instead of an integer, causing a stack overflow. This was such a unique corner case, we would not have considered testing for it. Additionally, even if we had considered it, running all our testing on different browsers with different localizations would have become cost prohibitive. It is issues like this that remind us that the DP is not complete until the new code has been monitored in production and is behaving as expected.

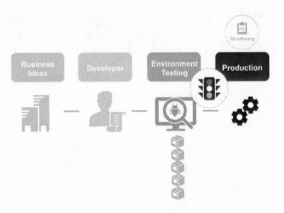

Summary

Understanding and improving a complex DP in a large organization can be a complicated process. Therefore, it makes sense to start by exploring a very simple DP with one developer and understanding the associated challenges. This process starts with the business idea being communicated to the developer and ends with working code in production that meets the needs of the customer. There are lots of things that can and do go wrong in large organizations, and the DP provides a good framework for putting those issues in context. In this chapter, we introduced the concept and highlighted some typical problems. Chapter 3 will introduce the DevOps practices that are designed to address issues at each stage in the pipeline and provide some metrics that you can use to target improvements that will provide the biggest benefits.

Chapter 3

OPTIMIZING THE BASIC DEPLOYMENT PIPELINE

Setting up your DP and using DevOps practices for increasing its throughput while maintaining or improving quality is a journey that takes time for most large organizations. This approach, though, will provide a systematic method for addressing inefficiencies in your software development processes and improving those processes over time. We will look at the different types of work, different types of waste, and different metrics for highlighting inefficiencies. We will start there because it is important to put the different DevOps concepts, metrics, and practices into perspective so you can start your improvements where they will provide the biggest benefits and start driving positive momentum for your transformation.

The technical and cultural shifts associated with this will change how everyone works on a day-to-day basis. The goal is to get people to accept these cultural changes and embrace different ways of working. For example: As an Operations person, I have always logged into a server to debug and fix issues on the fly. Now I can log on to debug, but the fix is going to require updating and running the script. This is going to be slower at first and will feel unnatural to me, but the change means I know, as does everyone else, that the exact state of the server with all changes are under version control, and I can create new servers at will that are exactly the same. Short-term pain for long-term gain is going to be hard to get some people to embrace, but this is the type of cultural change that is required to truly transform your development processes.

Additionally, there are lots of breakthroughs coming from the field of DevOps that will help you address issues that have been plaguing your organization for years that were not very visible while operating at a low cadence. When you do one deployment a month, you don't see the issues repeating enough to see a common cause that needs to be fixed. When you do a deployment each day, you see a pattern that reveals the things that need fixing. When you are deploying manually on a monthly basis, you can use brute force, which takes up a lot of time, requires a lot of energy, and creates a lot of frustration. When you deploy daily, you can no longer use brute force. You need to automate to improve frequency, and that automation allows you to fix repetitive issues.

As you look to address inefficiencies, it is important to understand that there are three different kinds of work with software that require different approaches to eliminate waste and improve efficiency. First, there is new and unique work, such as the new features, new applications, and new products that are the objective of the organization. Second, there is triage work that must be done to find the source of the issues that need to be fixed. Third, there is repetitive work, which includes creating an environment, building, deploying, configuring databases, configuring firewalls, and testing.

Since the new and unique work isn't a repetitive task, it can't be optimized the way you would a manufacturing process. In manufacturing, the product being built is constant so you can make process changes and measure the output to see if there was an improvement. With the new and unique part of software you can't do that because you are changing both the product and the process at the same time. Therefore, you don't know if the improvement was due to the process change or just a different outcome based on processing a different type or size of requirement. Instead the focus here should be on increasing the feedback so that people working on these new capabilities don't waste time and energy on things that won't work with changes other people are making, won't work in production, or don't meet the needs of the customer. Providing fast, high-quality feedback helps to minimize this waste. It starts with feedback in a production-like environment with their latest code working with everyone else's latest code to ensure real-time resolution of those issues. Then, ideally, the feedback comes from the customer with code in production as soon as possible. Validating with the customer is done to address the fact that 50% of new software features are never used or do not meet their business intent. Removing this waste requires getting new features to the customers as fast as possible to enable finding which parts of the 50% are not meeting their business objective so the organization can quit wasting time on those efforts.

In large software organizations, triaging and localizing the source of the issue can consume a large amount of effort. Minimizing waste in this area requires minimizing the amount of triage required and then designing processes and approaches that localize the source of issues as quickly as possible when triage is required. DevOps approaches work to minimize the amount of triage required by automating repetitive tasks for consistency. DevOps approaches are also designed to improve the efficiency of the triage process by moving to smaller batch sizes, resulting in fewer changes needing to be investigated as potential sources of the issue.

The waste with repetitive work is different. DevOps moves to automate these repetitive tasks for three reasons. First, it addresses the obvious waste of doing something manually when it could be automated. Automation also enables the tasks to be run more frequently, which helps with batch sizes and thus the triage process. Second, it dramatically reduces the time associated with these manual tasks so that the feedback cycles are much shorter, which helps to reduce the waste for new and unique work. Third, because the automated tasks are executed the same way every time, it reduces the amount of triage required to find manual mistakes or inconsistencies across environments.

DevOps practices are designed to help address these sources of waste, but with so many different places that need to be improved in large organizations, it is important to understand where to start. The first step is documenting the current DP and starting to collect data to help target the bottlenecks in flow and the biggest sources of waste. In this chapter we will walk through each step of the basic DP and will review which metrics to collect to help you understand the magnitude of issues you have at each stage. Then, we will describe the DevOps approaches people have found effective for addressing the waste at that stage. Finally, we will highlight the cultural changes that are required to get people to accept working differently.

This approach should help illustrate why so many different people have different definitions of DevOps. It really depends what part of the elephant they are seeing. For any given organization, the constraint in flow may be the planning/requirements process, the development process, obtaining consistent environments, the testing process, or deploying code. Your view of the constraint also potentially depends on your role in the organization. While everything you are hearing about DevOps is typically valid, you can't simply copy the rituals because it might not make sense for your organization. One organization's bottleneck is not another organization's bottleneck so you must focus on applying the principles!

Requirement/Planning

Here we are talking about new and unique work, not repetitive work, so fixing it requires fast feedback and a focus on end-to-end cycle time for ultimate customer feedback.

For organizations trying to better understand the waste in the planning and requirements part of their DP, it is important to understand the data showing the inefficiencies. It may not be possible to collect all the data at first, but don't let this stop you from starting your improvements. As with all of the metrics we describe, get as much data as you can to target issues and start your continuous improvement process. It is more important to start improving than it is to get a perfect view of your current issues. Ideally, though, you would want to know the answers to the following questions:

- *What percentage of the organizations capacity is spent on documenting requirements and planning?*

- *What is the amount of requirements inventory waiting for development, roughly, in terms of days of supply?*

- *What percentages of the requirements are reworked after origi-nally defined?*

- *What percentages of the delivered features are being used by the customers and are achieving the expected business results?*

Optimizing this part of the DP requires moving to a just-in-time approach to documenting and decomposing requirements only to the level required to support the required business decisions while limiting the commitment of long-term deliveries to a subset of the overall capacity. The focus here is to limit the inventory of require-ments as much as possible. Ideally this would wait until the devel-oper is ready to start working on the requirement before investing in defining the feature. This approach minimizes waste because effort is not exerted until you know for sure it is going to be developed. It also enables quick responsiveness to changes in the market because great new ideas don't have to wait in line behind all the features that were previously defined.

While this is the ideal situation, it is not always possible because organizations frequently need a longer-range view of when things might happen in order to support different business decisions. For example, you might ask yourself, "Do I need to ramp up hiring to meet schedule, or should I build the manufacturing line because a product is going to be ready for a launch?" The problem is that most organizations create way more requirements inventory a long way into the future than is needed to support their business decisions. They want to know exactly what features will be ready when using waterfall planning because that is what they do for every other part of the business. The problem is that this approach drives a lot of waste into the system and locks in to a committed plan what should be your most flexible asset. Additionally, most organizations push their software teams to commit to 100% of their capacity, meaning they are not able to respond to changes in the marketplace or discov-eries during development. This is a significant source of waste in a lot of organizations.

I have worked with one organization that moved to a more just-in-time approach for requirements and that has transformed their planning processes from taking 20% or more of their capacity to less than 5%. They eliminated waste and freed up 15% of the capacity of their organization to focus on creating value for the business. This was done by limiting long-term commitments of over a year to less than 50% of capacity and committing additional capacity in shorter timeframe horizons. The details of how this worked are in Chapter 5 of Leading the Transformation by Gary Gruver and Tommy Mouser. This was a big shift that freed up more capacity, and it also improved the speed of value through the system because new ideas could move quickly into development if they were of the highest priority instead of waiting in queue behind a lot of lower-priority ideas that were previously planned.

This move is a big cultural change for most organizations. It requires software/IT and business executives to think differently about how they manage software. They really need to change their focus from optimizing the system for accuracy in plans to optimizing it for throughput of value for the customer. They need to be clear about the business decisions they need to support and work with the organization to limit the investment in requirements just to the level of detail required to support those decisions.

Environments

For many organizations, like the one described in Chapter 2, the time it takes for Operations to create an environment for testing is one of the lengthiest steps in the DP. Additionally, the consistency between this testing environment and production is so lacking that it requires finding and fixing a whole new set of issues at each stage of testing in the DP. Creating these environments is one of the main repetitive tasks that can be documented, automated, and put under revision control. The objective here is to be able to quickly create environments that provide consistent results across the DP. This is done through a movement to infrastructure as code, which has the additional advantage of documenting everything about the environments so it is easier for different parts of the organization to track and collaborate on changes.

To better understand the impact environment issues are having on your DP, it would be helpful to have the following data:

- *time from environment request to delivery*

- *how frequently new environments are required*

- *the percent of time environments need fixing before acceptance*

- *the percent of defects associated with code vs. environment vs. deployment vs. database vs. other at each stage in the DP*

One of the biggest improvements coming out of the DevOps movement concerns the speed and consistency of environments, deployments, and databases. This started with Continuous Delivery by Jez Humble and David Farley. They showed the value of infrastructure as code, where all parts of the environment are treated with the same rigor and controls as the application code. The process of automating the infrastructure and putting it under version control has some key advantages. First, the automation ensures consistency across different stages and different servers in the DP. Second, the automation supports the increased frequency that is required to drive to smaller batch sizes and more frequent deployments. Third, it provides working code that is a well-documented definition of the environments that everyone can collaborate on when changes are required to support new features.

Technical solutions in this space are quickly evolving because organizations are seeing that getting control of their environments provides many benefits. Smart engineers around the world are constantly inventing new ways to make this process easier and faster. Cloud capabilities, whether internal or external, tend to help a lot with speed and consistency. New scripting capabilities from Chef, Puppet, Ansible, and others help with getting all the changes in scripts under source control management. There have also been breakthroughs with containers that are helping with speed and consistency. The "how" in this space is evolving quickly because of the benefits the solutions are providing, but the "what" is a lot more consistent. For environments, you don't want the speed of provisioning to be a bottleneck in your DP. You need to be able to ensure consistency of the environment, deployment process, and data across different stages of your DP. You need to be able to qualify infrastructure code changes efficiently so your infrastructure can move as quickly as your applications. Additionally, you need to be able to quickly and efficiently track everything that changes from one build and environment to the next.

Having Development and Operations collaborate on these scripts for the entire DP is essential. The environments across different stages of the DP are frequently different sizes and shapes, so often no one person understands how a configuration change in the development stage should be implemented in every stage through production. If you are going to change the infrastructure code, it has to work for every stage. If you don't know how it should work in those stages, it forces necessary discussions. If you are changing it and breaking other stages without telling anyone, the SCM will find you out and the people managing the DP will provide appropriate feedback. Working together on this code is what forces the alignment between Development and Operations. Before this change, Development would tend to make a change to fix their environment so their code would work, but they wouldn't bother to tell anyone or let people know that in order for their new feature to work, something would have to change in production. It was release engineering's job to try and figure out everything that had changed and how to get it working in production. With the shift to infrastructure as code, it is everyone's responsibility to work together and clearly document in working automation code all of the changes.

This shift to infrastructure as code also has a big impact on the ITIL and auditing processes. Instead of the ITIL processes of documenting configuration of a change manually in a ticket, it is all documented in code that is under revision control in a SCM tool.

The SCM is designed to make it easy to track any and all changes automatically. You can look at any server and see exactly what was changed by who and when. Combine this with automated testing that can tell you when the system started failing, and you can quickly get to the change that caused the problem. This localization gets easier when the cycle time between tests limits this to a few changes to look through.

Right now, the triage process takes a long time to sort through clues to find the change that caused the problem. It is hard to tell if it is a code, environment, deploy, data, or test problem. and currently the only thing under control for most organizations is code. Infrastructure as code changes that and puts everything under version control that is tracked. This eliminates server-to-server variability and enables version control of everything else. This means that the process for making the change and documenting the change are the same thing so you don't have to look at the documentation of the change in one tool to see what was approved and then validate that it was really done in the other tool. You also don't have to look at everything that was done in one tool and then go to the other tool to ensure it was documented. This is what they do during auditing. The other thing done during auditing is tracking to ensure everyone is following the manual processes every time–something that humans do very poorly, but computers do very well. When all this is automated, it meets the ITIL test of tracking all changes, and it makes auditing very easy. The problem is that the way DevOps is currently described to process and auditing teams makes them dig in their heels and block changes when instead they should be championing those changes. To avoid this resistance to these cultural changes, it is important to help the auditing team understand the benefits it will provide and include them in defining how the process will work. This will make it easier for them to audit, and they will know where to look for the data they require.

Using infrastructure as code across the DP also has the benefit of forcing cultural alignment between Development and Operations. When Development and Operations are using different tools and processes for creating environments, deploying code into those environments, and managing databases, they tend to find lots of issues releasing new code into production. This can lead to a great deal of animosity between Development and Operations. As they start using the same tools, and more specifically the same code, you will likely find that making the code work in all the different stages of the DP forces them to collaborate much more closely. They need to understand each other's needs and the differences between the different stages much better. They also need to agree that any changes to the production environments start at the beginning of the DP and propagate through the system just like the application code. Over time, you will likely find that this working code is the forcing function that starts the cultural alignment between Development, Operations, and all the organizations in between. This is a big change for most large organizations. It requires that people quit logging in to servers and making manual changes. It requires an investment in creating automation for the infrastructure. It also requires everyone to use common tools, communicate about any infrastructure changes that are required, and document the changes with automated scripts. It requires much better communication across the different silos than exists in most organizations.

Organizations doing embedded development typically have a unique challenge with environments because the firmware/software systems are being developed in parallel with the actual product so there is very little, if any, product available for early testing. Additionally, even when the product is available, it is frequently difficult to fully automate the testing in the final product. These organizations need to invest in simulators to enable them to test the software portions of their code as frequently and cheaply as possible. They need to find or create a clean architectural interface between the software parts of their code and the low-level embedded firmware parts. Code is then written that can simulate this interface running on a blade server so they can test the software code without the final product. The same principle holds true for the low-level embedded firmware, but this testing frequently requires validating the interactions of this code with the custom hardware in the product. For this testing, they need to create emulators that support testing of the hardware and firmware together without the rest of the product.

This investment in simulators and emulators is a big cultural shift for most embedded organizations. They typically have never invested to create these capabilities and instead just do big bang integrations late in the product lifecycle that don't go well. Additionally, those that have created simulators or emulators have not invested in continually improving these capabilities to ensure they can catch more and more of the defects over time. These organizations need to make the cultural shift to more frequent test cycles just like any other DevOps organization, but they can't do that if they don't have test environments they can trust for finding code issues. If the organization is not committed to maintaining and improving these environments, the organization tends to loose trust and quit using them. When this happens, they end up missing a key tool for transforming how they do embedded software and firmware development.

Testing

The testing, debug, and defect fixing stage of the DP is a big source of inefficiencies for lots of organizations. To understand the magnitude of the problem for your DP, it would be helpful to have the following data:

- *the time it takes to run the full set of testing*

- *the repeatability of the testing (false failures)*

- *the percent of defects found with unit tests, automated system tests, and manual tests*

- *the time it takes the release branch to meet production quality*

- *approval times*

- *batch sizes or release frequency at each stage*

The time it takes for testing is frequently one of the biggest bottlenecks in flow in organizations starting on the DevOps journey. They depend on slow-running manual tests to find defects and support their release decisions. Removing or reducing this bottleneck is going to require moving to automated testing. This automated testing should include all aspects of testing required to release code into production: regression, new functionality, security, and performance. Operations should also work to add monitoring or other operational concerns to these testing environments to ensure issues are found and feedback is given to developers while they are writing code so they can learn and improve. Automating all the testing to run within hours instead of days and weeks is going to be a big change for most organizations. The tests need to be reliable and provide consistent results if they are going to be used for gating code. You should run them over and over again in random order against the same code to make sure they provide the same result each time and can be run in parallel on separate servers. Make sure the test automation framework is designed so the tests are maintainable and triageable. You are going to be running and maintaining thousands of automated tests running daily, and if you don't think through how this is going to work at scale, you will end up dying under the weight of the test automation instead of reaping its benefits. This requires a well-designed automation framework that is going to require close collaboration between Development and QA.

It is important to make sure the tests are designed to make the triage process more efficient. It isn't efficient from a triage perspective if the system tests are finding lots of environment or deployment issues. If this happens, you should start designing specific post-deployment tests to find and localize these issues quickly. Then once the post-deployment tests are in place, make sure they are passing and the environments are correct before starting any system testing. This approach improves the triage efficiency by separating code and infrastructure issues with the design of the testing process.

Automated testing and responding to feedback is going to be a big cultural shift for most organizations. The testing process is going to have to move from manually knowing how to test the applications to using leading edge programming skills to automate testing of the application. These are skills that don't always exist in organizations that have traditionally done manual testing. Therefore, Development and the test organization are going to have to collaborate to design the test framework. Development is going to have to modify how they write code so that automated testing will be stable and maintainable. And probably the biggest change is to have the developers respond to test failures and keep build stability as their top priority.

If you can't get this shift to happen, it probably doesn't make sense to invest in building out complex DPs that won't be used. The purpose of the automated testing is not to reduce the cost of testing, but to enable the tests to be run on a more frequent basis to provide feedback to developers in order to reduce waste in new and unique work. If they are not responding to this feedback, then it is not helping. Therefore, it is important to start this cultural shift as soon as possible. Don't write a bunch of automated tests before you start using them to gate code. Instead, write a few automated build acceptance tests (BATs) that define a very minimal level of stability. Make sure everyone understands that keeping those tests passing on every build is job one. Watch this process very carefully. If it is primarily finding test issues, review and redesign your test framework. If it is primarily finding infrastructure issues, start designing post-deployment tests to ensure stability before running any system test looking for code issues. If it is primarily finding code issues, then you are on the right track and ready to start the cultural transformation of having the developers respond to feedback from the DP. The process of moving to automated tests gating code is going to be a big cultural shift, but it is probably one of the most important steps in changing how software is developed.

Testing more frequently on smaller batches of changes makes triage and debugging much easier and more efficient. The developers receive feedback while they are writing the code and engaged in that part of the design instead of weeks later when they have moved on to something else. This makes it much easier for them to learn from their mistakes and improve instead of just getting beat up for something they don't even remember doing. Additionally, there are fewer changes in the code base between the failure and the last time it passed, so you can quickly localize the potential sources of the problem.

The focus for automated testing really needs to be on increasing the frequency of testing and ensuring the organization is quickly responding to failures. This should be the first step for two reasons. First, it starts getting developers to ensure the code they are writing is not breaking existing functionality. Second, and most importantly, it ensures that your test framework is maintainable and triagable before you waste time writing tests that won't work over the long term.

I worked with one organization that was very proud of the fact that they had written over one thousand automated tests that they were running at the end of each release cycle. I pointed out that this was good, but to see the most value, they should start using them in the DP every day, gating builds where the developers were required to keep the builds green. They should also make sure they started with the best, most stable tests because if the red builds were frequently due to test issues instead of code issues, then the developers would get upset and disengage from the process. They spent several weeks trying to find reliable tests out of the huge amount available. In the end, they found out that they had to throw out all the existing tests because they were not stable, maintainable, or triagable. Don't make this same mistake! Start using your test automation as soon as possible. Have the first few tests gating code on your DP, and once you know you have a stable test framework, start adding more tests over time.

Once you have good test automation in place that is running in hours instead of days or weeks, the next step to enabling more frequent releases is getting and keeping trunk much closer to production-level quality. If you let lots of defects build up on trunk while you are waiting for the next batch release, then the bottleneck in your DP will be the amount of time and energy it takes to fix all the defects before releasing into production. The reality is that to do continuous deployment, trunk has to be kept at production levels of quality all the time. This is a long way off for most organizations, but the benefit of keeping trunk closer to production-level quality is worth the effort. It enables more frequent, smaller releases because there is not as big an effort to stabilize a release branch before going into production. It also helps with the localization of issues because it is easier to identify changes in quality when new code is integrated. Lastly, while you may still have some manual testing in place, it ensures that your testers are as productive as possible while working on a stable build. This might not be your bottleneck if you start with a lot of manual testing because the developers can fix defects as quickly as the testers can find them. However, this starts to change as you add more automated tests. Watch for this shift, and be ready to move your focus as the bottleneck changes over time.

This transition to a more stable trunk is a journey that is going to take some time. Start with a small set of tests that will define the minimal level of stability that you will ever allow in your organization. These are your BATs. If these fail due to a change, then job one is fixing those test failures as quickly as possible. Even better, you should automatically block that change from reaching trunk. Then over time, you should work to improve the minimal level of stability allowed on trunk by farming your BAT tests. Have your QA organization help identify issues they frequently find in builds that impact their ability to manually test effectively. Create an automated test to catch this in real time. Add it to the BAT set, and never do any manual testing on a build until the all the automated tests are passing. Look for major defects that are getting past the current BAT tests, and add a test to fill the hole. Look for long running BAT tests that are not finding defects, and remove them so you have time to add more valuable tests. This is a constant process of farming the BAT test that moves trunk closer to release quality over time.

If you are going to release more frequently with smaller batches, this shift to keeping trunk stable and closer to release quality is required.

It is also going to be a big shift for most organizations. Developers will need to bring code in without breaking existing functionality or exposing their code to customers until it is done and ready for release. Typically, organizations release by creating a release branch where they finalize and stabilize the code. Every project that is going to be in a release needs to have their code on trunk when the release branches. This code is typically brought in with the new features exposed to the customer ready for final integration testing. For lots of organizations, the day they release branch is the most unstable day for trunk because developers are bringing in last minute features that are not ready and have not been tested with the rest of the latest code. This is especially true for projects the business wants really badly. These projects tend to come in with the worst quality, which means every other project on the release has to wait until the really bad project is ready before the release branch can go to production. This type of behavior tends to lead to longer release branches and less frequent releases. To address this, the organization needs to start changing their definition of done. The code can and should be brought in but not exposed to the customer until it meets the new definition of done. If the organization is going to move to releasing more frequently, the new definition of done needs to change to include the following: all the stories are signed off, the automated testing is in place and passing, and there are no known open defects. This will be a big cultural shift that will take some time.

The final step in this stage of the DP is the approval for moving into production. For some organizations that are tightly regulated, this requires getting manual approval by someone in the management chain, which can take up to days to get. For organizations that are well down the path to continuous deployment, this can be the biggest bottleneck in the flow of code. To remove this bottleneck, highly regulated organizations move to have the manager who was doing the manual approval work with testers document their approval criteria with automated tests. For less regulated environments, having the developer take ownership and responsibility for quickly resolving any issues found in productions can eliminate the management approval process.

There are lots of changes that can help improve the flow at this stage of the DP. The key is to make sure you are prioritizing improvements that will do the most to improve the flow. So, start with the bottleneck and fix it, then identify and fix the next bottleneck. This is the key to improving flow. If your test cycle is taking six weeks to run and your management approval takes a day, it does not make any sense to take on the political battle of convincing your organization that DevOps means it needs to let developers push code into production. If, on the other hand, testing takes hours, your trunk is always at production levels of quality, and your management approval takes days, then it makes sense to address the approval barriers that are slowing down the flow of code. It is important to understand the capabilities of your organization and the current bottlenecks before prioritizing the improvements.

Production Release

The next step in the basic DP is the release into production. Ideally, you would have found and fixed all the issues in the test stage so that this is a fairly automated and simple process. Realistically, this is not the case for most organizations. To better understand the source and magnitude of the issues at this stage, it is helpful to look at the following metrics:

- *the time and effort required to deploy and release into production*

- *the number of issues found during release and their source (code, environment, deployment, test, data, etc...)*

If you are going to release code into production with smaller more frequent releases, you can't have a long drawn out release process requiring lots of resources. Many organizations start with teams of Operations people deploying into a datacenter with run books and manual processes. This takes a lot effort and is often plagued with manual errors and inconsistencies. DevOps addresses this by auto-mating the release process as the final step in the DP. The process has been exercised and perfected during earlier stages in the DP and production is just the last repeat of the process. This automa-tion ensures consistency and greatly reduces the amount of time and people required for release.

The next big challenge a lot of organizations have during the release process is that they are finding issues during the release process that they did not discover earlier in the DP. It is important to understand the source of these issues so the team can start addressing the rea-sons they were not caught before release into production. As much as possible, you should be using the same tools, processes, and scripts in the test environment as in the production environment. The test environment is frequently a smaller version of production, so it is not exact, but as much as possible you should work to abstract those differences out of the common code that that defines the environ-ment, deploys the code, and configures the database. If you are find-ing a lot of issues associated with these pieces, start automating these processes and architect for as much common code across the DP as possible. Also, once you have this automation in place, any patches for production should start at the front end of the pipeline and flow through the process just like the application code.

Organizations with large complex deployments also frequently strug-gle with the triage process during the launch call. A test will fail, but it is hard to tell if it is due to an environment, deployment, database, code, or test issue. The automated testing in the deployment process should be designed to help in this triage process. Instead of config-uring the environments, deploying the code, configuring the data-base, and running and debugging system tests, you need to create post-deployment automated tests that can be run after the environ-ments are configured to make sure they are correct server by server. Do the same thing for the deployment and database. Then after you have proven that those steps executed correctly, you can run the sys-tem tests to find any code issues that were not caught earlier in the DP. This structured DevOps approach really helps to streamline the triage process during code deployment and helps localize hard to find intermittent issues that only happen when a system test happens to hit the one server where the issue exists.

Making these deployments into production work smoothly requires these technical changes, but mostly it requires everyone in the DP working together to optimize the system. This is why the DP is an essential part of DevOps transformations. If Operations continually sees issues during deployment, they need to work to design feedback mechanisms upstream in the DP so the issues are found and fixed during the testing process. If there are infrastructure issues found during deployment, Operation teams need to work with the Development teams to understand why the infrastructure as code approaches did not find and resolve these issues earlier in the DP. Additionally, the Operations team should be working with the test organization to ensure post-deployment tests are created to improve the efficiency and effectiveness of the triage process. These are all very different ways of working that these teams need to embrace over time if the DevOps transformation is going to be successful.

Operation and Monitoring

The final step is operating and monitoring the code to make sure it is working as expected in production. The primary metrics to monitor here are:

- *issues found in production*

- *time to restore service*

Some organizations are so busy fighting issues in production that they are not able to focus on creating new capabilities. Addressing production quality issues can be the biggest challenge for these organizations. In these situations, it is important to shift the discovery of these issues to earlier in the pipeline. The operational organization needs to work with the development organization to ensure their concerns and issues are being tested for and addressed earlier in the pipeline. This includes adding tests to address their concerns and adding monitoring that is catching issues in production to the test environments. As discussed in the release section, it also requires getting common tools and scripts for environments, deployments, and databases across the entire DP.

Implementing all these changes can help ensure you are catching most issues before launching into production. It does not necessarily help with the IE8 issue with Spanish localization discussed in Chapter 2. In that case, it would have just been too costly and time consuming to test every browser in ever localization for every test case. Instead, the other significant change that website or SaaS type organizations that have complete control over their deployment processes tend to implement is to separate deployment from release by using approaches like feature toggles and canary releases. This enables new versions of the system to be released into production without new features being accessible to the customer, a pattern known as "dark launching." This is done due to the realization that no matter how much you invest in testing, you still might not find everything. Additionally, the push to find everything can drive the testing cost and cycle times out of control. Instead these organizations use a combination of automated testing in their DP and canary releases in production. Once the feature makes it through their DP, instead of releasing it to everyone at once, they do a canary release by giving access to a small percentage of customers and monitoring the performance to see if it is behaving as expected before releasing it to the entire customer base. This is not a license to avoid testing earlier in the pipeline, but it does enable organizations to limit the impact on the business from unforeseen issues while also taking a pragmatic approach to their automated testing.

Summary

This simple construct of a DP with a single developer does a good job of introducing the concepts and shows how the DevOps changes can help to improve flow. The metrics are also very useful for targeting where to start improving the pipeline. It is important to look across all the metrics in the DP to ensure you start this work with the bottleneck and/or the biggest source of waste because transforming your development and deployment processes is going to take some time, and you want to start seeing the benefits of these changes as soon as possible. This can only occur if you start by focusing on the biggest issues for your organization. The metrics are intended to help identify these bottlenecks and waste in order to gain a common understanding of the issues across your organization so you can get everyone aligned on investing in the improvements that will add the most value out of the gate.

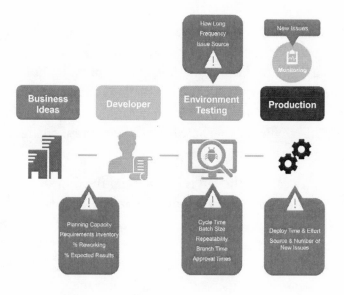

Chapter 4

SCALING TO A TEAM WITH CONTINUOUS INTEGRATION

Continuous integration is the first step in the DP if you have more than one developer. This is the first thing that changes with the DP when you start scaling beyond one developer to a team of developers, and it drives lots of changes in behavior. All the different developers bring their code together and make sure it is working. You need to make green builds job one and develop in a way that allows you to bring code in without breaking trunk. This is a big change for developers used to traditional methods, but it provides huge advantages. Until you have done it, you can't imagine that it will ever work, but once you have done it this way, you can't imagine working any other way. The challenge is ensuring that the cultural changes occur and that the teams are embracing this new way of working.

The first step in scaling the DP is broadening the flow of work from one developer to a team working on an application. The big change here is associated with distributing the development across members in the team and then integrating all their changes to ensure it all works together, meets the business expectations, and does not break existing functionality. This requires improving the communication with the business and across team members, which is usually accomplished with Scrum practices. It also requires implementing continuous integration, where developers are frequently checking code into trunk and responding to test failures, as the first step towards delivering code in the DP.

Scaling to CI

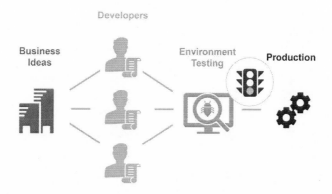

To understand the impact of this additional complexity on top of the basic DP it is helpful to understand the following additional metrics:

- *number of green builds a day and the percent green in continuous integration*

- *time to recover from a red build*

- *percent of features requiring rework before acceptance by the business*

- *amount of effort required to integrate code from different developers to complete a working feature*

These last two metrics are a big source of waste that the Agile-Scrum process is designed to address. Scrum makes all the different developers on a team have a quick meeting every morning with the business lead. This helps to ensure that the developers create what the business wants and ensures that the developers are talking about how all their code is going to work together. If these two metrics are your biggest issues, then by all means start with Scrum. If not, maybe start somewhere else. As we talked about in Leading the Transformation, how the teams work is the second order effect. How the teams come together to deliver value is the first order effect. Continuous integration or stage 1 of the DP is the forcing function that aligns the team.

Further integration in all the stages that follow are the forcing function that aligns across teams. This merge and integration of the code early and often is what helps to minimize rework waste.

If when scaling the DP to a team the last two metrics stand out as your biggest sources of waste, then bringing in an Agile coach to work with the team should be one of your highest priorities. The Scrum process and daily standups are designed to improve alignment across team members and with the business. There is a lot of great material from the Agile community to help with these improvements, so it won't be repeated here. The point, however, is to put those changes and improvements in perspective as part of the broader DP so organizations understand the waste being targeted with those improvements and the magnitude of those issues within the broader perspective of the flow of value through the organization.

If instead the first metric or others from Chapter 3 stand out as the biggest issues when scaling the pipeline across a team, it probably make sense to focus on those. From a development perspective, having continuous integration in the DP drives significant changes in how developers need to work on a day-to-day basis. Continuous integration is used to quickly find and resolve issues where different developers on the team are making changes that won't work together or won't work in production. It requires that the developers make keeping the build green their top priority and that the operation people ensure the issues they are concerned about are represented with automated tests in the continuous integration environment. It also requires developers checking in their code to trunk on a regular basis instead of allowing it to stay out on branches and in dedicated environments. This is a big cultural change for most organizations and a completely different way of working, but it is probably the most foundational piece of DevOps and the DP. If you can't get the organization to make the shift to integrating code on trunk and keeping it stable, you are going to be limited in your ability to improve the flow and release more frequently.

Continuous integration also requires a significantly different approach to development to enable bringing in new code without breaking the existing functionality. In the past, the team members would work together on a dedicated branch, coordinating changes across the application, services layer, and database, then, when everything was together and working, it would be merged to trunk.

This front end branching enabled the teams to develop and make sure everything could work together without breaking trunk. The problem was that once all the changes were ready, you had to merge this big batch of changes with all the other changes that had occurred on trunk since the branch was created. This merge process can tend to be difficult and delay the discovery of code on the different branches that would not work together. It also drives inefficiencies in the development process because it allows developers to keep working on code separately that won't work together and requires duplication of effort on both branches.

Therefore, there is a strong drive to move away from branching in your DP. This requires new approaches for the Development team. Instead of coordinating changes across the application and services layer, the team needs to move to approaches like versioning the services so the application and services layer can independently bring changes to trunk without breaking the build. Instead of modifying a service to support the new feature, add version two of the service that supports the new feature on trunk. Then the application can bring in the new code when it is ready and call the version of the code it needs for the feature. The test framework should be able to test both the new feature and the old feature on trunk at the same time while the old feature is toggled on in the trunk environment. Then, after the testing on the new feature is passing and using the new version of the service, trunk can toggle from the old feature to the new feature, and the old version of the service can be deprecated. A similar approach needs to be taken for database changes using the techniques described by Scott Ambler and Pramod Sadalage in their book Refactoring Databases. There are lots of reasons development teams will give for why they must branch, but you should understand that all these issues have been solved by other organizations to enable them to optimize flow in their DP. Getting developers to make these changes is going to require technical solutions, but mostly it is about leading the cultural changes of getting them to work differently on a day-to-day basis.

Summary

Continuous integration is the first step in scaling the DP beyond one developer. It is also one of the most important first steps in finding waste and inefficiencies in your software development and delivery processes. It forces the organization to debug and deal with instabilities in the system by requiring them to keep the builds green. It is this process that starts providing insights into the biggest issues for the organization. Are the builds failing due to code, environments, deployments, test problems, or data? The answers to these questions are critical to understanding what changes will help address the biggest sources of waste that exist in your organization. However, this requires a big cultural shift to ensuring everyone is focused on keeping the build green as their top priority. It also requires developers to embrace different approaches to coding so they can continually bring changes to trunk without breaking existing functionality.

Chapter 5

SCALING BEYOND A TEAM

Most large organizations start DevOps with a small prototype. They work to improve part of a DP or a full DP for a smaller application. They see all the advantages it provides for that team and decide that they would see much bigger benefits if they scaled it across the entire organization. They approach it focused on trying to figure out how to get everyone to do DevOps exactly the same way they did it in the small prototype, and they try to create a company-wide centralized plan for the change. This approach, however, overlooks organizational change management, which is the biggest challenge. When driving change, it is harder to get people to comply with your wishes than it is to help them create and own their plans, which is the key factor in ultimately making those plans successful. Additionally, the challenges that they are facing with their DP are frequently very different from the challenges found in the prototype and, thus, require different solutions.

It is much easier to get people to own leading the cultural changes when the plans are their own and they have the flexibility to prioritize the improvements that will help their business the most. Instead of getting lost in the rituals, which happened in a lot of Agile transformations, the focus needs to be on helping them learn how to apply the principles. Forcing them to change and do things simply because they are being told to, doesn't work. At HP, we were very focused on the principles and gave the teams as much flexibility as possible in terms of how they worked. They had the ownership and made their approaches successful. I am seeing too many DevOps implementations overlook this point and focus on creating a common plan for everyone; a bottom up approach has some success, so they want to scale by telling everyone to do it that way (rituals instead of principles). But teaching them the principles and helping them create a plan that will make their own work successful, is the way to go. Providing a framework that traditional organizations can use to create their plan and align the organization under the plan is essential. That, and allowing people to say "no" to changes they are hearing about that were designed for coordinating work of tens of people that won't work well for coordinating the work of hundreds. Right now, everyone is hearing about different DevOps ideas. They are all good, but nobody is putting them in context. Most importantly, there needs to be differentiation between what applies to tens of people versus what applies to thousands.

The first step for large organizations is segmenting the problem into smaller, more manageable pieces with local ownership focusing on areas where the changes can add the most value. Changing how a large organization works is hard enough without making it bigger and more complex than is required. The more developers and operational people that have to work together, the more complicated it gets. Therefore, you should break out different parts that don't have to be developed, tested, and deployed as a unit because the architecture is tightly coupled. For example, in retail where companies are trying to create common experiences at every customer interface, creating the capability to buy online and pick up in store requires coordinating the work across large, tightly coupled systems. It impacts the website and mobile teams for ordering. It goes through credit and inventory systems that are typically on legacy systems. Then it goes through the point of sales systems and tools for the stores. These systems are so tightly coupled that moving to buy online and pick up in store requires coordinating the development, testing, and deployment across all those systems. In this case, that is one DP. The HR system is not coupled, so it should be treated as a separate DP. The purchasing and ordering systems are not coupled, so they could also be a different DP.

This segmentation approach is a bit different from the bi-modal DevOps approach that is currently being discussed in the industry where the recommendation is just to use DevOps for the front-end systems of engagement and use more traditional approaches for the systems of record. The idea behind bi-modal is that you should apply DevOps on more modern applications that have the DevOps type of tooling in place and leave the old, complex, legacy applications alone. The theory is that this approach also enables fast changes at the customer interface where they are most important for delivering value. This is a nice simplifying approach if it works, but my experience is that changing the customer experiences frequently requires changing both systems of engagement and systems of record. Therefore, you need to improve the flow of change through all the systems that need to work together, which is why I recommend defining and optimizing based on the entire DP.

Segmenting the problem into as many independent DPs as possible is the first step, and allows you to define and optimize the DP for each one separately. The next step is to determine which DPs are worth the investment to optimize. If the DP for certain applications, such as the HR system, are not core to how you compete and are not being updated much, it is probably not worth the investment.

Segmenting

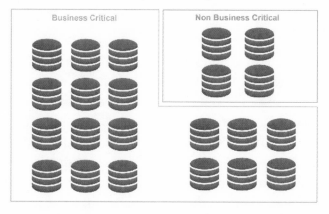

If the applications are worth the investment, it becomes essential to make the DP as small as possible for a few reasons. Coordinating less people is easier than coordinating more, especially in software. Different DPs will have different sources of waste and cycle time. This process will take some time, so you will want to start where you see the biggest benefits for your effort to get positive momentum. Most importantly, since this is all about getting people to change how they are working on a daily basis, you will want people to take ownership for making their ideas successful. If the leaders of that DP have the latitude to prioritizing the things that will benefit their DP the most, then they will make their ideas successful, and they are likely to fix their biggest issues. If this DP can be simplified down to small teams of 5 to 20 people, you can implement the DevOps practices in one way because people can wrap their mind around the complete system and take ownership.

If the smallest the DP can get is thousands of people, then you have to take different approaches. DevOps thinking spends so much time hearing about the improvements from small teams that the differences between approaches aren't well appreciated. DevOps thinking tends to look at this from the perspectives of small teams and from the bottom up. As an executive trying to change large, tightly coupled systems, I have a different view of the world. Ideally everyone should architect for small independent teams because they will always be more efficient, but the reality is that it is hard and takes time, so you probably need to improve the process while you are waiting for re-architecture efforts by optimizing the current DPs.

DevOps forces the coordination across lots of different people and departments, including: multiple Development teams, Development, QA, Security, and Operations. DevOps improvements can help small teams significantly, but the opportunities for improvement are much larger for larger teams just because there are so many more opportunities for misunderstandings between people. Coordinating the work across large organizations is more difficult, and if you simply try to use the same improvement processes that worked for small teams, you won't get the same successful results. Since many DevOps thinkers have not led a transformation at scale, it is understandable that they don't appreciate the differences. Additionally, most of the people leading the DevOps movement are from new, leading edge companies that have architectures that enable them to work independently. They don't understand what it takes to coordinate the work of hundreds or thousands of workers, or the benefit that different approaches can provide. Instead of asking these large, tightly coupled organizations to behave like loosely coupled organizations, we should be talking about the complex systems they have and helping them figure out how to deliver code on a more frequent basis while maintaining all aspects of quality. They need a framework for understanding what they should be doing to get everyone in a large organization on the same page. Telling them that what they need to do is have Development push code to production at will is doing them a disservice. Telling them they need to solve problems with thousands of people the same way you solve them for small teams is wrong. Dealing with large, complex systems requires a different approach, and if done well, the opportunities for improvements are much greater because the inefficiencies associated with developing code across more people is much larger.

Scaling across a large organization requires segmenting the DPs into two different types because the approaches taken will be different. The first group consists of applications where fairly small teams can independently develop, qualify, and deploy code and where they don't have to share significant code with other groups. Think micro-services or Amazon service-oriented architectural approaches that allow small teams to work independently. The second group consists of larger applications or groups of applications where larger groups of people need to work together to develop, qualify, and deploy code because of tight coupling in the architecture. This group probably needs to include code that is common and needs to be shared across groups. Ideally, every application would fit in the first loosely coupled architectural grouping since smaller, less complex things are easier to manage and improve. The reality for most large, traditional organizations, however, is that a lot of the code architecture is tightly coupled or needs to be shared, and you can't ignore that complexity.

Segmenting

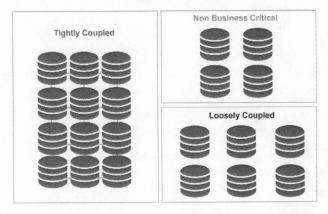

Given this complexity, the next step is to take the applications that are tightly coupled and form them into the groups that have to be developed, qualified, and deployed as a system. Next, examine each of the groupings to see if there are fairly easy architectural changes that you can make that enable you to break the system into two smaller, more manageable chunks. This is an important step before starting to optimize the DPs because managing and improving smaller systems is much less complex than doing the same for the larger ones, and it enables more localized ownership to make it successful.

Breaking the problem down into smaller more manageable chunks is going to be challenging for organizations with tightly coupled legacy architectures. It is also going to be difficult for very large organizations that share a common core set of code across lots of businesses. In these cases, you are going to have to find a pragmatic approach that can help simplify and segment the problem as much as possible. If you have a very large, tightly coupled architecture, can you start with a smaller component in the system? If you have common code leveraged across lots of very large businesses, can you create a plan for that common code and how it is delivered to the businesses instead of lumping all the businesses into a common plan? It is going to be hard to change a large organization. Therefore, it is going to be important to simplify and segment wherever possible. Once you have identified the large, tightly coupled systems that are key to the business and can't be broken down any smaller, it is time to start setting up and optimizing the DP.

Summary

Organizational change management is the biggest challenge when scaling DevOps across an entire organization. I find it is much easier to get people to own leading the cultural changes if they have the flexibility to prioritize the improvements that will help their business the most and if the plans are their own. The focus then becomes helping these people learn how to apply the principles and develop their plans. This starts by creating manageable pieces with local ownership that can focus on changes that will add the most value for that specific DP. It also requires being clear about the size and complexity of the DP because coordinating work across large and small teams is different.

Chapter 6

SCALING WITH LOOSELY COUPLED ARCHITECTURES

Scaling DevOps in large organizations with loosely coupled architectures is more about propagating the teams and approaches in parallel across the organization as depicted in the graphic below. In this chapter, we will discuss the cultural changes at the team level, the removal of barriers, and the placing of any guardrails for the team. Culturally, you want the team to feel ownership and responsibility all the way from the business idea to working code in production that meets the need. You want to remove barriers by providing capabilities on demand that will support the needs of the teams and help break down cross-organizational barriers. These teams should be allowed as much flexibility as possible in determining how they meet those objectives so they take ownership for the success. In large organizations, though, it frequently makes sense to have some commonality. It is important to be clear about where and why these common guardrails may exist.

Loosely Coupled

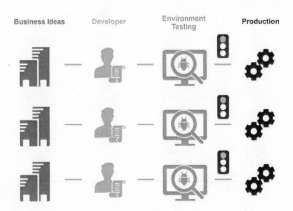

Cultural

The nice thing about having an architecture that enables small teams to work independently is that they can learn, adapt, and respond more quickly than large, complex, tightly coupled systems. They are also typically close enough to all the work going on with the team that they can understand and respond to most issues. In these cases, you are trying to reinforce and support team ownership for the success of the project and extend it all the way out to working code in production. This requires integrating quality, security, performance, and operational perspectives into the Development team and breaking down the silos between different organizations. This process is significantly different if you are working in a tightly coupled architecture, which will be covered in the next chapter.

It is helpful in these situations to reinforce ownership by having everyone on the team take turns wearing the pager for off-shift support rather than having separate operational support. There is nothing like needing to personally get up at 2:00 AM to make you think through whether the new feature is ready to release into production on a Friday afternoon. And there is nothing like having to work through production issues to help you understand how to write code that will work in production and how to provide the monitoring in the code that will make it easier to debug production issues. This is at the core of the "you build it, you run it" mentality at Amazon, Google, and other large, fast moving organizations. This is also behind the two pizza team rule at Amazon where they work to keep teams and services small enough that the team members can understand the system and have that personal level of ownership. This cultural end-to-end view of the product is at the core of these teams learning and adapting, which enables them to move faster. To support this learning you need to create a blameless culture where people feel comfortable sharing failures so everyone can learn from the mistakes.

The ability of these small independent teams to move fast and learn is at the core of the movement to micro services. There are other architectural approaches that enable small teams to work independently, but this is the most popular one at the moment. The idea is to encapsulate everything required for the service to run in a micro service that can be updated independently without breaking the broader application. It is so much easier for these small, independent teams to move fast that wherever possible you should make the architectural changes to support this approach. This can be through the current popular micro services approach or other architectural techniques that enable independence between teams.

Barriers

The other important aspect to enabling these teams to move fast is to start removing barriers that would slow down and frustrate them. Focus on providing them with the resources they need and removing the bureaucracy that exists in most large organizations. These teams should not have to wait on slow moving central organizations to provide them with what they need. They also should not have to go through slow moving approval processes.

There is nothing more demoralizing for these small, fast moving teams than having to wait to get an environment to test a new feature or to wait for an environment in production where they can deploy the code. Success in these situations really requires being able to provide environments with cloud-like efficiencies on demand for testing and production. Teams also need to have access in test environments to the production monitoring capabilities so they can ensure the application is ready and has the appropriate monitoring working for debug of production issues. The infrastructure needs to easily support canary releases so they can experiment quickly without putting the entire customer base at risk. The leadership team needs to work to ensure the infrastructure and tools are in place to support the teams so they can focus on delivering business value.

The leadership team also needs to help by removing bureaucracy and organizational barriers that exist in most large traditional organizations. The change approval boards that exist in organizations, which don't really understand the changes the teams are implementing, need to be replaced with more efficient processes. The barriers and division of responsibilities across Development, QA, Security, and Operations need to be knocked down to enable efficient collaboration. Processes that were put in place for a command and control approach need to be redesigned or eliminated to support the culture of empowerment and accountability at the team level.

Guardrails

While moving quickly with empowered teams and letting them make their decisions is important for organizations with loosely coupled architectures, it might not be possible or practical to give them complete independence. As you start scaling these teams across the organization, it will be important for everyone to understand where they have independence and where they need to use common tools or share common processes.

For example, in tightly regulated industries, if you are going to remove bureaucratic processes like the change approval board, you need to ensure there are some auditable standards for moving changes into production. Do you require the previous approver with separation of duties to codify their approval criteria in automated tests that enables auditable release criteria with the speed these small fast moving teams require? Do you require canary releases to less than X% of customers to run for Y time before complete release into production? Leaders are going to have to help drive these types of changes because they are big, cross-organizational changes not successfully driven at the team level. That said, once the changes are in place, the teams will have to work within the guidelines that have been defined if the organization is going to pass the audits required for regulatory approval.

There are other places where the teams might want to take advantage of the efficiencies of working in a large organization. For example, do you want to empower every team to pick their own tools for scripting environments and deployments, or do you want to have a

common approach and more common environments to enable efficiencies and leverage across the organization? This is a more difficult decision because it walks the line between empowerment and
efficiencies. Ideally, this wouldn't be a hard and fast rule. Instead,
infrastructure and capabilities would be put in place to make using
the common tools and approach the path of least resistance so teams
naturally pick them if they meet their needs.

For practical reasons, large organizations may need to consider other
commonalities across teams to enable efficiencies in procurement
and the ability to look across the organization. For example, all the
code at Google is in one of two SCM tools where anyone can check
out and look at the code at any time. Teams cannot choose whether
to use a different SCM or make their code available. This takes away
from the team's independence in some respects, but they decided
that the tradeoff was worth the advantage of having common tools
that enabled collaboration across the company. Organizations may
or may not want to consider similar commonality for looking at
demand in business requirements across teams. This commonality
can be driven by the ability to work across teams, or it may be driven
by the costs of buying tools and the efficiencies of enterprise licenses.

Summary

For large organizations with loosely coupled architectures, scaling DevOps is more about cultivating the teams and approaches in
parallel across the organization. Small teams are able to work independently, and unlike in large, complex and tightly coupled system,
they can learn, adapt, and respond more quickly. Create a blameless
culture where failures are shared, and everyone learns from mistakes.
These small independent teams can move fast and learn fast. Start
removing barriers that will slow and frustrate the teams, and remove
bureaucracy and organizational barriers that exist in most large
traditional organizations. There is a lot of value in empowering the
teams so they own the success of their approach. There are also valid
reasons for driving some level of consistency across large organizations. As organizations start scaling these small, fast-moving teams,

it is important for the leadership teams to think through these issues and be clear about what if any guardrails they are going to require.

Chapter 7

DOCUMENTING THE DEPLOYMENT PIPELINE FOR TIGHTLY COUPLED ARCHITECTURES

Documenting and optimizing the DP for tightly coupled architectures is an important concept and what all of this book's chapters have been leading up to. We have built the foundation and put everything into context so you can determine how to handle the complexity of large systems and appreciate the differences from DevOps for small independent teams. For tightly coupled architectures that require hundreds or even thousands of engineers to coordinate the development, qualification, and deployment of code, the DP gets more complex. One way to try to work with this complexity is to have one big continuous integration process on the front end of the pipeline where everyone checks in and does multiple builds a day. A complex enterprise system can take a long time to deploy, however, and automated testing for everything on that complex of an environment can take a while. It can result in builds with changes from too many developers, which makes it challenging to localize the issues during the triage process and hard to keep the builds green. So it is important when designing complex DPs to break the design down into more manageable pieces. This can be done by increasing the build frequency, reducing the test time by running a subset automated testing defined as BAT, and using service virtualization to break the system into smaller more manageable pieces. Once you have these smaller, more manageable pieces you take the basic construct of continuous integration and expand it into the integration of stable subsystems that build up into the enterprise system with appropriate automated quality gates.

The first step in designing the DP for a large, complex, tightly-coupled system is to draw up the architecture with all the applications showing the couplings and interfaces. If you can build, deploy, and run a reasonable set of BAT tests on the system frequently enough to have a small enough number of changes that triage is efficient, then you should use one large continuous integration process for the entire system.

Tightly Coupled Architecture

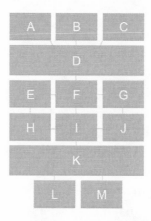

If you can't build frequently enough to keep the number of commits small, which is typical of large complex enterprise systems, think about how to break this up into smaller, more manageable pieces. Look for clean interfaces where it would be easy to mock the interface with service virtualization. Ideally, you would not need this step at all because maintaining the service virtualization is going to take some effort. Therefore, you should avoid the step where possible by just using build frequency to localize the offending code, but when the build time of this complex system takes too long or there are just so many developers working on the system that you have over 20 commits per build, it probably makes sense to break it up into smaller subsystems that you can keep stable for integration. When breaking it down, look for opportunities to reduce the number of commits per build where there are natural organizational and architectural interfaces.

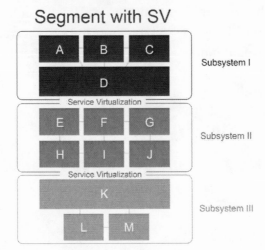

Once the subsystems that can be optimized based on build frequency are defined, you need to define the DP for building each of them. This should start with continuous integration or stage 1 of the DP for each application, with each team owning their component with a quality gate for keeping major issues out of the subsystem build. This gate at each stage will be defined by a subset of BATs that will define the minimal level of stability that you will ever allow in the system.

Next, the DP should take the latest green builds out of each of the components and build those into a subsystem with automated subsystem BAT testing running against the service virtualization as many times a day as possible. Stage 2 of the DP is really continuous integration of the components of continuous integration that have to work together running the subsystem BAT. Stage 3 takes the latest green build each day out of stage 2 and runs the full set of automated regression tests. This step is designed to catch issues that slip past the BAT. If you see major drops in the regression passing rates for a build, then you should fix the defect and add a test from the regression suite to the BAT set. This process of always evaluating and improving your BAT is how you work to improve the stability of trunk over time.

Subsystem I Deployment Pipeline

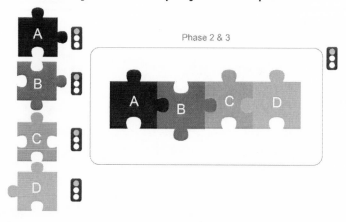

Keeping this code base up and running with green builds at this subsystem level should be the top priority for everyone in this part of the organization. Creating subsystems around natural organizational boundaries where possible helps by providing clarity in responsibilities for keeping these subsystems stable. Having BAT gates at each stage helps keep the large systems as stable as possible while localizing the ownership for fixing issues to the teams that created the problem. These subsystems are then built and tested in the full system without virtualization as frequently as possible, using BAT testing in stage 4 and then full regression in stage 5 before going into production. This is ideally how code should flow through your system. It is nice to start with the end point in mind.

Full System Deployment Pipeline

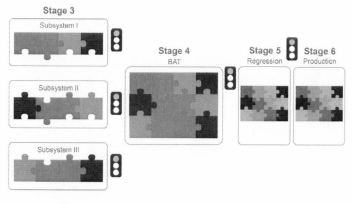

Next, understand how your current DP works. You may not call it a DP, but there is a process for how you build up, test, and release these large enterprise systems. It is important for the organization to understand how that works before you start making improvements. From a similar perspective, starting at the developer committing code, determine the steps for building up and testing this system Draw it up on a wall and get people together to review it for accuracy. This will have a lot more complexity than the simple construct described in Chapters 2 and 3, but the concepts are similar. Once you have completed this map, you have a first pass at your DP.

Summary

We have shown how to create a DP for a large tightly coupled architecture. It starts by breaking the system into smaller, less complex components and subsystems that can be kept stable with appropriate build acceptances tests for quality gates. Next, it involves building up these smaller pieces into the larger, more complex, stable systems on a regular basis. This approach helps to localize the identification of issues as early in the DP as possible to improve the efficiency of the triage process and reduce the feedback time for developers. It also documents how code flows from a business idea to production for complex systems, which is the first step to understanding the processes that need to be improved. Now you are ready for Chapter 8, where we will start optimizing the complex DPs described here.

Chapter 8

OPTIMIZING COMPLEX DEPLOYMENT PIPELINES

Everything up until this point has given us the context we need to optimize complex DPs. We understand the basic framework of the DP with metrics for one developer and how DevOps practices address those issues. We have covered how Development needs to change how they work in order to make continuous integration work. We have segmented down to the big, complex, hard-to-solve problems. We have acknowledged that loosely coupled architectures are best and that a lot of what you are hearing about DevOps mostly applies to them. And we have an early view of complex DPs. Now we are ready to deal with the complexity of large, tightly coupled systems. It is time to get everyone to agree on the biggest issues so we can start making improvements. It is with this macro view of the elephant that you start achieving the organizational alignment you need to move forward in a coordinated fashion.

DevOps helps to improve the productivity of software organizations because it starts to address the inefficiencies between people, teams, and organizations. It also helps improve the effectiveness of individuals by improving the quality and frequency of feedback. The biggest opportunities for improvement, though, are across the organization, which is more important for large, complex DPs. It also helps for small, independent teams as discussed in Chapter 6, but since there are less people to coordinate for these organizations, the impact of the improvements on productivity will be less dramatic. These smaller teams will always be more nimble and able to deploy more frequently because they are dealing with less complex systems, which is why you should re-architect for independence whenever possible. That said, the biggest inefficiencies in most large organizations exist in the large, complex, tightly coupled systems that require coordination across large numbers of people from the business all the way out to Operations.

Waste in Large Organizations

As we are trying to improve the frequency of release with quality (DevOps) in large organizations, we need to reduce cycle time, remove duplicate work, and eliminate waste so things can move more quickly. It helps to understand the types of work and inefficiencies you are trying to address to help facilitate this quickness.

Product owners responsible for representing the needs of the business can experience a lot of waste in the DP. They spend time documenting requirements that are misunderstood by Development and Test teams. They spend time documenting requirements that the Development teams are never able to implement. They work on features that the customers won't use or don't meet the need of the business. They spend time prioritizing and re-prioritizing features that never get developed. They waste time trying to sign off on features in test environments where the code was not correctly deployed or where the environment is unstable.

Developers waste time working on new features that do not meet the expectations of the business. They waste time creating code that does not work with features being created by others. They waste time building new code on top of recently created defects because of slow feedback from testing. They waste time creating features that will never be used because it takes too long to get the minimal viable product in front of customers. They waste time triaging defects that were thought to be code but ended up being issues with data, environments, and deployments. They end up debugging and fixing the same defect more than once because all the right fixes are not correctly committed to all the right branches. They waste time localizing issues among hundreds of changes to find out the defect was with someone else's code and not their own.

The testing process wastes time creating and executing tests that were not designed as the business or the developer had in mind. The QA organization wastes time and energy testing on a build that has the wrong version of code, is in an environment that is not configured correctly, or is unstable for other reasons. This leads to wasted effort documenting defects that are not repeatable, which leads to ongoing debates between Development and QA. In organizations that use branching, QA spends a lot of time testing the same code and finding the same defects on two different branches of the code.

The release team wastes time trying to find all the right versions of the code and the proper definition of the environments, and getting all the right data in place to support testing. In fact, lots of organizations spend more time and effort getting the big, complex enterprise environments up and ready for testing than they do actually writing the code. They find out tests fail because one group overwrote the data another group needed for testing. They find out tests fail because the developer did not let them know they needed a patch in the OS, or a firewall opened to support the new features. These types of waste and inefficiencies can make it very difficult to release code, which leads to infrequent releases and large batch sizes.

Operations is the last stage in the DP, but it can also be a large source of waste. If there are a lot of defects being released into production, they end up spending most of their time just firefighting. If Development teams are not clearly communicating the changes they are making or are not providing instrumentation in their code for efficient debug, it is very hard to keep the applications up and running.

Executive Lead Continuous Improvement

Addressing these inefficiencies and getting the organization focused on improving the biggest issues in the DP requires looking across the system and prioritizing improvements. The challenge is getting the organization to agree on the biggest sources of waste so you can start a focused continuous improvement process. This effort needs to be led by a person or group of people that are chartered to own the overall process. Because it requires looking across different groups in the organization, this tends to be an executive or team of executives that come together to lead the transformation. They need to be able to prioritize improvements across the teams that will add the most value. They also need to ensure everyone is supporting the changes the team has decided to implement.

However, this can't be an executive directed initiative because the executives don't really understand the problems well until they spend time out in the organization getting a better feel for the issues in the system. It needs to be more of an executive lead approach where they are spending time out in the organization understanding issues, prioritizing improvements, and helping to remove barriers. It starts with the executives working with the organization to agree on a common set of prioritized improvements that will have the biggest impact on the business for the first iteration, which is the goal of this framework. Then, during the iteration, the executives need to spend time out in the organization to understand what is and isn't getting done. Most importantly, they need to understand why these prioritized improvements aren't getting done because that starts to highlight the improvements that should be prioritized for the next iteration. This progress should be reviewed with a checkpoint at the end of each iteration to review what got done, what didn't get done, what was learned, and what are the deliverables for the next iteration. It is this ongoing, continuous improvement effort that coordinates the improvement efforts. For more details see Leading the Transformation by Gary Gruver and Tommy Mouser.

The first step in leading the transformation is getting the technical and managerial team together to gain a common understanding of the biggest sources of waste and inefficiencies in the system (a common view of the elephant). This analysis should be done for each DP by the people responsible for working on those applications. The team needs to start with the architecture and work through the process defined in Chapter 7 to document a common understanding of how the DP works. Next, we will walk through the metrics the team should work to capture for the DP to give everyone a common understanding of the biggest sources of waste and inefficiencies that should be addressed. The goal of this exercise is to agree on the objectives for the first monthly iteration. The intent is to identify tangible work that the team feels can and should be completed in the next 30 days—in other words, work that will help the organization the most. There are four types of metrics in addition to the ones reviewed in Chapter 3 that are important to these more complex DP that we will describe next. The team should populate their DP and discuss the issues before agreeing on the objectives for the first month. Again, don't worry about getting the metrics perfect or accurate to three significant digits. The goal here is to provide enough metrics that the organization can agree on the biggest sources of waste so they know where to start the continuous improvement process.

Mapping Waste Associated with Duplicate Work

The first step in identifying waste and opportunities for improvement in the DP is to look for duplication of work. If you are using branching extensively, this is probably one of the biggest sources of wastes. This usually happens with different branches of code where you are either duplicating the entire DP or significant portions of it. This can be due to branching during the release process where you isolate to drive to production-level stability or for product organizations to support a variety of products. Either way, it forces duplication of work in the system. Developers need to ensure they are committing the correct code to the branches where it is required and not to the ones where it isn't. Testing needs to occur on both branches, which can be really problematic and expensive if there is any manual testing left in the system. Additionally, branching drives duplicate efforts in debugging and triaging defects. Therefore, branches should be seen as a source of waste if they are very long lived and require a significant amount of effort to support. In the beginning, they usually exist for a reason, but as you start working to improve your development and deployment processes, you should look to address those reasons so the duplicate work associated with branches can be minimized.

Release Branching Duplicate Work

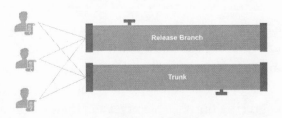

The other place that branching and duplication of work tends to occur is in product development organizations with embedded firmware. Here duplication of work is associated with getting the code up and running and qualified on the different products that frequently have hardware differences. To minimize this waste it is important to either minimize the hardware variability or architecturally isolate these differences from as much of the common code as possible. The architecture should be designed to have small components that are unique for specific products to deal with the hardware differences and should be minimized as much as possible. When possible, components that are common but need to behave differently for different products that need to leverage code should not be branched because of the duplication of work. For these components, instead of embedding all the product differences in the component, there should be a file that contains the product differences in one place that is referenced by the component code. Lastly, there is platform code that should be common across all the products that should not branch.

Release Branching Duplicate Work

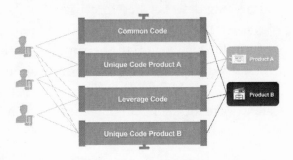

Mapping Cycle Time and Batch Sizes

The next step in analyzing the DP is to evaluate it for cycle time and batch sizes. DevOps is all about increased frequency, which is enabled by shorter lead times and smaller batch sizes. Shorter cycle times and smaller batch sizes help with rework waste from slow feedback, and smaller batch sizes also help with triage efficiency. Cycle time and batch sizes are typically driven by repetitive work or fixing defects before release. You should start the automation of repetitive work where it will have the most benefit for cycle time. Cycle time is important because it drives feedback times to minimize the amount of work on features that customers won't use, that won't work with other code, or that won't work in production. The reduction in cycle time minimizes the time different groups across the DP invest in things that won't work together. They can then identify the issues and ensure those issues are addressed as soon as possible.

The reduction in cycle time will also help to reduce the batch size, which makes triage in large, complex systems simpler because there are fewer changes since the last time the tests were passing. To reduce cycle time, you are going to have to automate long running manual processes, such as testing, and manual processes that are painful, but that you would like to do more frequently, such as deployment. Automating these repetitive tasks is required not only to reduce the cycle time, but also to make small batch sizes with simpler triage affordable. It has the added benefit of eliminating errors that frequently occur with manual processes. When you focus on reducing cycle time with smaller batches, it also forces you to fix issues that have been plaguing your organization for years. When you were not building, deploying, testing, or releasing as frequently, your organization could not see the issues as repetitive, and it was just muscling its way through the issues every time. As you start increasing the frequency, this is not possible. You have to start understanding and addressing these issues and fixing them with automation where possible.

Cycle Time and Batch Size Map

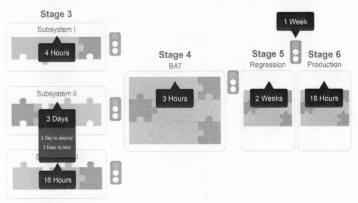

This example of a cycle time map, while simplified to major subsystems, does help to target major bottlenecks. It shows stage 4 taking three hours, which is pretty good, but subsystem II is stuck at three days with one day to deploy and two days to test. This would be a good target for improving cycle time with some deployment and test automation. Additionally, if the deployment into production is taking a large group of people 18 hours, you are not going to want to release more frequently until those issues are addressed.

Mapping Types of Issues

Next, we need to look at the DP map in terms of the kind of issues we are seeing at each stage because the type of issues will define what we start fixing first. With this map we are really trying to separate the new/unique work issues from issues caused by repetitive work because the solution for these types of issues will be different. Additionally, we want to understand the type of repetitive issues we have so we know what to prioritize fixing. The errors in repetitive work are addressed with automation, which also helps with cycle time. To understand which repetitive work in the DP should be prioritized for fixing, you should look at the cycle time and type of issues map to determine where to start. Additionally, if a significant portion of your issues are non-code related, you are going to want to automate your testing in ways that will make your triage process more efficient. Instead of just building an environment, deploying code, configuring data, and running system tests, start using post-deployment validation steps at the end of each step to ensure the step was completed successfully and is ready for code testing. Then, when you run the system tests you can find code issues instead of starting a long, drawn out triage process across code, environments, deployments, and data.

Source of Issue Slide

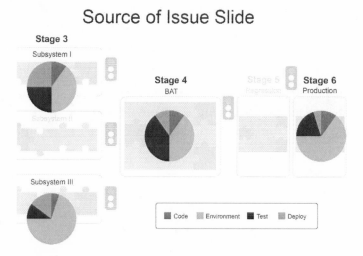

This example map shows that code is not a significant part of the problem. In this case, if you were to start your DevOps journey by gating code for your developers, you would not be very successful. The developers would start by responding to all the failures, but once they spent time debugging and realized that the issues weren't very often associated with their code, they would disengage from responding to the feedback, and your transformation would falter. Instead, in this example the team should focus on automating their environments and getting those definitions under version control so the environment issues are not overwhelming the DP. Next, they would need to address the consistency of the test automation because if these tests can't be used as a reliable gate for catching code issues, they are not very helpful.

Mapping Sources of Code Issues

Code issues are new and unique work. The key here to removing waste lies in minimizing the time spent working on code that does not work together, does not work in production, and does not meet the business intent. You want to find these issues as quickly as possible to minimize waste. You also want to minimize the impact of these defects on the rest of the system. This is done by reducing cycle time and gating defects from impacting the stability of the system. The cycle time map will be used to drive feedback frequency. Mapping the sources of code issues will help you understand how to prioritize creating or improving quality gates. These quality gates are a really important part of improving efficiencies in large, complex systems. These gates push the ownership for triaging and solving the issues to the people who created the problem and, more importantly, they improve the stability of the larger complex system so it is easier to triage. You should start with the subsystem that is leading to the most code defects and create a code gate for that application or subsystem. Start at the last integration point before production and work your way backwards, creating gates and making the system more stable.

Source of Code Defects

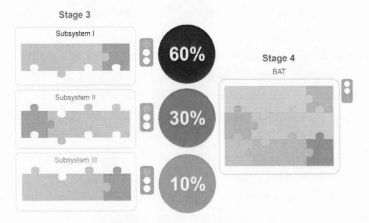

This example of the source of code defects shows that the majority of the defects in stage 4 are coming from subsystem I. It would be nice to automate the testing and gates for every subsystem from the start, but that is just not realistic for most organizations. This map shows that you should prioritize investments in automated testing and improving the gates for subsystem I because it is causing the most issues. Next, move onto subsystem II when you have the bandwidth or it becomes the next biggest source of issues. It is this process of prioritizing test automation and gates for continuous improvements that provides code that is more stable on an ongoing basis and is closer to release quality for more frequent releases.

This new and unique work for software will always be code but for embedded systems this gating is potentially new hardware and firmware subsystems that are not ready for product integration. Here, it is important to create gates in your product development life cycle to ensure these subsystems are ready before committing to using new HW on the platform. This requires a longer-range view of the DP, but the basic principle of gating instabilities from impacting the broader system applies.

The other big source of inefficiencies in the time to find code issues is front-end branching. This is where different teams each take a branch to create new capabilities. They work on the branches until the new features are ready and stable and then they integrate them on trunk. The problem with this way of working is that different teams on different branches don't see the interactions between the new code they are creating until it is merged to trunk. As we discussed in Chapter 4, moving away from this method is a big cultural change for most organizations, but it is also a big source of waste in most big, complex systems.

Putting It All Together

The graphics and metrics presented in this chapter can show additional complexities that are important to think about with tightly coupled systems. Ideally, you would want your team to have their entire DP mapped out on the wall, including as many of the metrics from this chapter and Chapter 3 as possible. It is this macro view of the elephant that you can use to get your organization aligned on where to start. The executives need to have the team review the mapping of all the metrics on your DP and see if you can get everyone to agree on the biggest issues and where to start.

When you are working on this alignment, it is very important to ensure that you have a repeatable process for gating code. The following questions are formulated to help you on that path:

- *For each stage in the DP do you have a stable environment for gating code?*

- *Are the automated tests reliable, maintainable, and triagable?*

- *Can you run all the tests multiple times in random order and get the same answer?*

- *Can you redeploy the same code and run the same tests and get the same answer? If not, do you need to start by focusing on the test and or environment/deployment issues?*

- *Are there certain applications that cause most of the defects in the enterprise system integration? Should you look at gating those applications first?*

- *How long does it take to build each stage of the pipeline?*

- *How long does it take to test each stage of the DP?*

- *What is the source of defects at each stage in the DP?*

In Chapter 3, we talked about capturing the source of issues based on code, environment, deployment, data, or tests. In more complex systems like this with integration points, it is also important to understand the source of the code defects in terms of the contributing subsystem. This becomes really important in large, complex organizations. Getting everything about environments, deployments, tests, and databases (repetitive work) automated is going to take time. You want Development and Operations starting the automation in the areas where you are seeing the most issues or longest cycle times across the DP. If your big issues are code, you work on gates with test automation at integration points starting with the source with the most code issues. If your biggest issues are repetitive tasks, you start with automation where it adds the most value in terms of repeatability and speed.

Summary

The process outlined in this chapter is going to take some time and be a journey for the organization. It is important to get everyone aligned so you are going through the journey as a team. There will be missteps and mistakes along the way, but if it is the team's plan, they will make it successful. The important part is getting them to agree on where to start and to be willing to engage with the team on the journey. I would recommend against planning this effort too far into the future because everyone is going to learn a great deal about what needs to be changed as they start implementing improvements. As I work with organizations, they frequently find that what they initially felt was the biggest issue was just the first layer of the onion. In these cases, if they had created a long term plan for improvement, it would have required a complete rework of the plan when they discovered the next layer of the onion. Instead, up front, work to get agreement across the business that you will invest X% of your capacity for these improvement efforts, then get started with the continuous improvement process using your map of the DP as the guide. This enables you to optimize complex DPs. Now that you understand this level of optimization, it is essential to look at the practices for tightly versus loosely coupled architectures.

Chapter 9

PRACTICES FOR TIGHTLY VERSUS LOOSELY COUPLED ARCHITECTURES

First, I want to acknowledge that everything you are hearing about DevOps practices are correct, but a lot of it best applies if you have 10 to 20 person problems. The perspective you have on DevOps and how to improve flow in your organization is going to depend largely on the size of the organization and the coupling in your architecture. We have covered a lot of the differences so far, but they are profound enough that it makes sense to review the biggest differences and why they exist in a more sustained and detailed way.

Executive Leadership versus Empowerment

For organizations with small teams that can work independently, the executive's role is less critical. These teams can come together with grass roots efforts to improve the way they develop, qualify, and deploy code on their own. They may need some roadblocks removed and some support, but the role of the executive is not as critical.

For large, complex systems, this is not the case. You need an executive or a team of executives to look over the creation and optimization of the DP to ensure everything is working well together and that parts of the organization aren't sub-optimizing the system to implement their view of DevOps. It needs to be the executive's plan, and they need to own it when working with the organization to prioritize and implement changes so that they also take ownership for making it successful. It also needs to involve ongoing work with the team to understand what is working and what needs to be improved next. Without this ongoing engagement, you are much more likely to create a DevOps elephant that has all the right parts, but doesn't look like or work like the elephant the business needs. That is going to require a person or team to constantly look at how the code is flowing through the system, analyze it for waste, and work with the team to prioritize the improvements. This is going to be a journey that is somewhat unique for each DP, which is going to require leaders who are willing to engage in the details of the process and guide the efforts.

Production Deployment

Saying that DevOps requires developers to push code into production without any approvals is a classic example of how understanding how DevOps is used in loosely coupled architectures and applying that to tightly coupled architectures is not the best practice. In organizations with loosely coupled architectures, one person can understand the entire application and fix it quickly if it fails in deployment. These organizations can also test in hours and have trunk at production-level quality. For them, waiting for the approval is the long lead time item. For most enterprises starting DevOps, the approval time is so far down the pareto chart that it is hard to see why you would even bother. Current DevOps thinking says that in order to do DevOps, developers must be able to push into production. This flies in the face of ITIL with separation of duties, and it is a nightmare to audit for regulated groups. People hear this and say, "Well, if that is DevOps, I can't do DevOps because I am regulated. Besides, when the ITIL process people or auditors hear this, they will throw up all sorts of roadblocks." As a result of this attitude, DevOps thinking is fighting an industry battle to get people to agree that separation of duties is not a requirement for regulatory so that enterprises can do DevOps. This is a misguided fight. It misses the point.

DevOps thinkers are getting so caught up in this debate that they are ignoring the six weeks it takes to test the code and get it production ready. There are so many other things these organizations can be doing to remove waste and increase the frequency of deployments without taking on this political battle that won't provide much benefit. The large, tightly coupled organizations would be better served by mapping their complex DPs and working to address the waste and inefficiencies that exist in their organization than by saying they must do X to be doing DevOps. The executives need to be actively engaged in this process to ensure the changes being implemented in the organization are providing the most value instead of fighting political battles that won't help much. Getting everyone to embrace these new ways of working is going to be challenging. It is going to require the executives' commitment to leading the change, which will require prioritizing changes that will improve the flow of value through the system, not just "doing DevOps."

Additionally, in small teams when the developers are pushing code into production, the likelihood that someone they don't know about is pushing in conflicting code changes at the same time they are, is fairly low. If there are hundreds of developers working on a tightly coupled system who can independently deploy code whenever they like, the likelihood of finding issues in production goes way up. Therefore, it does not make sense to have developers pushing directly into production. Instead, in large systems the developers should check code into the SCM once they feel it is ready and the right level of pretesting has been completed. After that, the DP is automatically kicked off with the continuous integration process to find and resolve conflicts in preproduction test environments. The DP then moves this code together with all the other changes through each stage of the DP. If a quality gate fails, then the developers in that batch need to respond and react to the failure, but they are not responsible for deploying the code into production. The deployment into production is the job of the automated DP. This is very different from loosely coupled systems, where developers independently push into production, but it is required when you are trying to coordinate the work across hundreds instead of tens.

Environments

The requirements for environments are a bit different for small teams versus complex systems. For small teams, the environments close to the developers are much more similar to the production environments because their code is much more encapsulated. For large tightly coupled systems, the developers often don't understand the complexities of the production environments. Additionally, the people that understand the production environments don't understand well the impact of the changes that developers are making. There are also frequently different end points in different test environment at each stage of the DP. No one person understands what needs to happen all the way down the DP. Therefore, managing environments for complex systems requires close collaboration from every group between Development and Operations.

This collaboration is much more effective if the deployment process and environments are under version control where everyone can see exactly who changed what and when. It is also more important that everyone understands how a change to these environments is going to be qualified to ensure it works with every stage in the DP. This is less important for small teams with less complexity and fewer stages between development and production. These small teams are more concerned about consistency across the DP and speed. This has some implications for the move to containers. They provide a significant quick win for small teams because they can move very fast and get the consistency they require. The containers also provide significant advantages for complex environments by encapsulating the complexity of the deployment and environment definition, but these teams will need to make sure the definitions of the containers are well documented and tracked in the SCM for collaboration. Additionally, they will need to think through what is changing and how they qualify changes to ensure they work at each stage in the DP.

There is another difference for environment availability for the complex DP. In the basic construct, you are concerned about how long it takes to provide a developer with an environment for testing before pushing code into production. You need environments on demand so developers are not waiting and can validate their changes easily so they catch their own defects. This requires an environment. In large, complex systems, once developers think code is ready, instead of pushing into production, they should just commit it to the SCM. The DP pipeline then monitors the SCM for changes and kicks off builds that flow through the DP. This creates an additional need for environments to support the DP. You need the ability to set up these environments easily, but once this is done, it is not really an environment-on-demand situation. It needs to be rebuilt on a regular basis with the latest definition of infrastructure as code, but the demand of DP environments should not be that variable. This may help to address the concern some large organization have that DevOps means giving production-level access to developers and letting them commit code. With a well-defined DP that is not the case. The pipeline deploys into product as long as the code meets all the gating requirements defined in terms of automated tests by the current approvers.

This automated DP pipeline can also cover the concerns with the approval process when that becomes the bottleneck, which tends to be more important in large complex organizations. In this case, instead of removing the separation of duty and all of those concerns, simply have the person responsible for the approval process describe the criteria they use for approval so you can create an automated test to represent their signoff. This approach has a few advantages. First, it forces more rigor into a somewhat arbitrary "management approval" process; they have to be clear about the criteria. Second, this approval process is documented in the SCM with an automated test so everyone can see and suggest modifications if required. Third, it is fast and automated by the DP so nobody is waiting around for manual approvals.

Quality Gates

For tightly coupled organizations, it is more important to build up stable enterprise systems using a well-structured DP with good quality gates. Before the transformation, many of these organizations spend a lot of time and effort setting up very complex enterprise test environments where they do the majority of their testing. These large test environments can be very expensive and hard to manage, so they are not a very efficient approach for finding defects. For these organizations, it is much more important to push the majority of testing and defect fixing down into smaller, less complex test environments with quality gates to keep defects out of the bigger more complex environments. This helps to reduce the cost and complexity of the testing. It also helps with the triage process because the issues are localized to the subsystem or application that created them. These types of issues really don't apply to loosely coupled organizations where the DP does not have to pass through these complex test environments. In these situations it is more practical to quickly and easily deploy code into production and then use techniques like canary releases to provide quick feedback to developers on small changes.

In large, tightly couple systems, the automated system testing becomes much more important. With loosely coupled systems, quick running unit tests can frequently find most of the issues. With tightly coupled systems, by definition, that is not the case. It requires creating effective system tests that can quickly find the unknown consequences of a change.

The small teams with decoupled architectures are also frequently working on relatively new applications where the code was written when unit testing was the expectation or where the application is still small enough that it is possible to add the required unit test coverage. This is frequently not the case with large, tightly coupled, legacy applications, where unit tests don't exist and you can't justify the investment to go back and add them. In these situations, it is much more important to start automating your current manual testing, which is frequently at the system level. If the tests are important enough to run manually, they are important enough to automate so you can eliminate the time and expense of the manual execution. It does, though, make sense to review the tests before automating to see if they can be eliminated because they are no longer valuable. However, the primary goal is going to be creating enough automated testing to turn off the manual tests so you can go faster and then over time plugging holes in the testing with more automation as defects make it to the next stage in the DP.

Specialization versus Generalist

For organizations with small teams that can work independently, it makes sense for the team to take end-to-end ownership for the system. This tends towards an emphasis on the generalist who can cover the process from business idea to supporting it in production. This approach tends to break down when the system gets so big and complex that not everyone on the team can understand the system. Here it makes more sense to have more specialization. For example, having developers wear pagers and not having a DevOps team, is a trend toward generalization. This works well for small teams because when the developer is paged out, the service they are supporting is small enough that they probably know what to fix or at least who to call to get help. It is also easy for that small team to add some Operations perspective to the groups to figure out how to own their service end to end.

This is not the case when you have hundreds or thousands of people working in a tightly coupled system. If a developer is paged out to fix a problem, the likelihood that it is due to code they know anything about is pretty low. It may create some empathy for what Operations is dealing with, but they aren't very likely to be in a position to help. Additionally, adding an Operations person to the Scrum team in a tightly coupled system may help with environments or a simple continuous integration process, but they are not likely to design, create, maintain, and optimize a large complex DP. This is going to take more of a structured effort with specialization. It could be led by Operations, Development, QA, Release, or a DevOps team, but someone is going to have to play that role.

Green Builds

When dealing with small teams, their ability to recover from red builds is probably more important than keeping the build green. They should not be so afraid of breaking the build that they spend too much time and effort before every commit making sure it is perfect. They should be able to use the infrastructure of the DP to provide that feedback as long as they are reacting to the feedback quickly and getting back to green. This applies to small teams that can work independently, but it also applies to stage 1 continuous integration in tightly coupled systems. As long as the teams can get back to a good build quickly and do so without impacting too many people, it makes sense to leverage the infrastructure of the DP. This, though, starts to change as you get further down more complex DPs. It starts impacting more people, and there is the potential for a lot of different people to break the build. In these situations, it is much more important to keep the builds green so code can successfully flow through the system. The more people it impacts and the longer it takes for a build and test cycle, the more important it is to catch the issues further up the DP where the impact can be localized.

Summary

The general DevOps principles are the same for large and small DPs—it is the practices that differ depending on the size. In principle, DevOps is all about how to improve the frequency of deployment while maintaining all aspects of quality, which requires coordinating work across people. As outlined here, however, the practices that you use for coordinating the work across tens of people versus hundreds of people can and should be different. Understanding these differences prepares you to understand the impact of the movement to DevOps in more complex, larger organizations and the approaches you should use.

Chapter 10

THE IMPACT OF MOVING TO DEVOPS IN LARGER, MORE COMPLEX ORGANIZATIONS

Once all the changes we have discussed in this book are in place, they can have a dramatic effect on how the business works. They impact how we manage software development, how we run the ITIL process, and how we do auditing.

Large software projects are hard to manage. It is difficult to coordinate the designs and work across different Development teams that have code that has to work together. Traditional organizations put lots of meetings and checkpoints in place to coordinate this work. This is especially important if the development organization is geographically dispersed and even more so if there are different contractors working on the code. The inefficiencies and waste associated with trying to understand and coordinate this work can be huge. Once you have a well-structured, rigorous DP in place, you will find that the working code is the forcing function that aligns and coordinates all this work. The teams and different contractors all need to be checking in their code on a regular basis to ensure it all works together, and they must be responsible for resolving those issues real-time if they are going to make it through the quality gates. You will find with the DP that working code is the forcing function that aligns all these different Development teams. The same thing happens when all the different organizations, from Development through Operations, are using infrastructure as code to coordinate their work. That working code becomes the forcing function that gives those teams the common objective of keeping the code working in a production-like environment. The other big change is that holding big meetings, or Scrum of Scrum meetings, become less important because everyone can watch the working code progress down the DP to understand status.

The area where there are big changes with the ITIL processes are for configuration management. With ITIL, any changes to production configurations were manually documented in change management tracking tools, manually approved by management, and manually implemented. With a rigorous DP, all that tracking, documenting, and implementation is all automated, and the changes are tracked in the source control management tool that is designed for tracking changes. The implementation uses this documented automation code to make any changes, ensuring what we said was going to happen actually happened like we said it would. Additionally, it requires that the approval processes that used to be arbitrary management decisions are documented with automated tests that support more repeatable and rigorous criteria for release.

This fundamental shift to a DP provides significant improvements in the auditing and compliance processes required for most organizations. Previously, conducting an audit required working through a sampling of change tickets to see if the appropriate people had approved the change before it went into production and making sure that the change implemented was actually what had been approved. This is what happens before creating a rigorous DP. Validating compliance requires auditing a small sample of the change requests to ensure everyone in the organization followed the process and manually going through different systems to pull data to show the process was followed. After the automated DP is in place and everything is automatically documented, it is much easier to ensure that the process is correctly followed for every change. This approach really takes advantage of what computers do very well, which is to repeat the same thing, the same way every time. The automation may initially be wrong, but once you get it fixed, you can count on it being done the same way every time, which is something very difficult to get humans to manually implement. The changes and criteria for approval are also automatically documented in the SCM tool where it is very easy for the auditors to see exactly who changed what and when. It is a huge improvement for both the efficiency and effectiveness of auditing, but it is also a big change. Therefore, it is important to include the auditors early in the process. Help them understand how this is going to help them do their job better and include them in the process so they can help define what data they need and where it will be kept. This is about organizational change management with the auditors too, so it important to include them in the plans so they will own making their ideas successful.

Moving to DevOps for large, tightly coupled organizations is a big job. It requires addressing waste and inefficiencies that have existed in your organization for years. The DP with the framework and metrics provided, though, provides a systematic approach for getting everyone one on the same page for optimizing the entire system. DevOps practices provide techniques for addressing waste to improve deployment frequency while maintaining all aspects of quality. The principles are the same across large and small teams, but the practices can and should be different.

In large, complex systems, it is important for the executives to pull the technical and managerial leaders for a DP together and to get everyone to agree on where there are the biggest opportunities for improvement. They need to kick start and lead the ongoing continuous improvement process. By following this process and using the DP framework provided by Jez Humble and David Farley, they can align the organization on a common plan that will result in a high performing DevOps elephant. This journey is going to take time and require that the executives engage with the teams to prioritize improvements to address waste and inefficiencies that have existed in most organizations for years, but if these companies expect to survive in industries where competition is being defined more and more by software, their software development and delivery processes must be improved.

BIBLIOGRAPHY

Lean Enterprise: How High Performance Organizations Innovate at Scale; Jez Humble, Joanne Molesky, and Barry O'Reilly

A Practical Approach to Large-Scale Agile Development; Gary Gruver, Mike Young, and Pat Fulghum

Toyota Kata: Managing People for Improvement, Adaptiveness, and Superior Results ; Mike Rother

Cucumber & Cheese: A Tester's Workshop; Jeff Morgan

Continuous Delivery: Reliable Software Releases through Build, Test, and Deployment Automation ; Jez Humble and David Farley

Refactoring Databases: Evolutionary Database Design; Scott W. Ambler and Pramod J. Sadalage

Leading the Transformation "Applying Agile and DevOps Principles at Scale"; Gary Gruver and Tommy Mouser

Implementing Lean Software Development: From Concept to Cash; Mary and Tom Poppendieck

Value Stream Mapping: How to Visualize Work and Align Ledership for Organizational Transformation; Karen Martin and Mike Osterling

The Phoenix Project: A Novel About IT, DevOps, and Helping Your Business Win; Gene Kim, Kevin Behr, and George Spafford